In the Foothills of Home
(Memories of growing up in the shadow of the Blue Ridge)

By H Wayne Easter

On the chance my great great grandchildren could someday know how old Pa Pa lived back in the Stone Age, I began jotting down some memories of growing up during the Great Depression. With pencil in hand I dived in and made so many mistakes, most of it landed in the trashcan.

Then, along came a new-fangled thing called a computer and I could make twice as many mistakes twice as fast, but amazingly, I could correct them. This book is the result. It has not been professionally edited and was written the way I thought it sounded best. An occasional mistake may still be found, but I hope you enjoy my trip down memory lane, to a time that will *not* come our way again.

Copyright © March 2014
All rights reserved
H. Wayne Easter
Mt Airy N C

Preface

Progress came late to the foothills of the Blue Ridge and as God intended, we followed the almanac and moon signs, plowed the Earth, sowed the seeds and literally dug a living from the rocky hillsides and creek bottoms. Hard times were normal times and when the Great Depression came calling, nothing changed; we just kept digging.

Owning almost nothing, my parents married in 1931 and eked out a living as sharecroppers in the fields of neighbors. In 1936, they built a one-room log cabin a half-mile west of Stewart's Creek, as Mama told it, "On a dry ridge way out in the middle of nowhere." As the years passed, the family increased, more rooms were added and for some 48 years, it was home for my parents and five boys.

We had fields of our own, but continued sharecropping until 1945 when we bought a neighbor's farm at auction. When electricity came over the hills in 1948, we bought our first car and those two events threw us kicking and screaming into a Twentieth Century already half gone. We never looked back.

Found in the following pages are some time-dimmed thoughts and memories of growing up in northwest Surry County N C. Included are some 140 plus photographs, drawings and crude maps of where and how we lived worked and played. Also included are chapters about my parents, grandparents, school, making moonshine, the great outdoors, the four seasons and how they ruled our lives.

With the selective memory of advancing years, I remember childhood as being at least as great as it was, if not better. We had no close neighbors and no one cared who rambled where in the huge backwoods. A brand new sun came up over Dave Carson's bottoms each morning, bringing brand new adventures in brand new lands. Armed with .22 rifle, homemade telescope and trusty Barlow, almost all of my free time was spent exploring the creek banks, bluffs and bottoms along my own raging river: Stewart's Creek.

There was so much to see and do and each new day brought more new questions, but that was no great problem; the days, weeks and years would never stop coming and someday I'd grow up and have all the answers. It has yet to happen, but maybe tomorrow------?

Stewart's Creek

Contents

Chapter:	Part 1	Page,
1-The Beginning		1
2-Exploring		9
3-Daydreams		19

Part 2

4-The Road to Home		27
5-Home		37
6-The Home Place		45

Part 3

7-Kermit and Elizabeth Easter		57
8-George and Alice Easter		67
9-The George Easter Home Place		77

Part 4

10-School		91
11-Winter Crop		97
12-Work and Play		103

Part 5

13-Winter		117
14-Spring		125
15-Summer		135

Part 6

16-Fall		145
17-Late Fall		155
Epilogue		163

Part 1

Wagon train on the Lambsburg Road (1971)

Fisher's Peak, seen from Tony Holder Road

Sam's Knob on Chestnut Grove Road near Lambsburg, Virginia

Chapter 1

The Beginning

Sugar Loaf Mountain

No one was here to see the beginning of this rocky hill country, a time when earthquakes and storms threw fire into the sky: when all the Heavens burned and new oceans boiled into being, as new mountains climbed out of the deep; where other mountains stood yesterday and still others would stand tomorrow. When Fisher's Peak and Sugar Loaf Mountains finally settled into their present forms, mankind was still in the far distant future.

At an unknown time, life began in the Earth, as rivers and streams found their way to the sea. From high on a mountaintop, two small streams began long downhill journeys through rock cliffs and laurel thickets. They splashed out of the mountain into an area now called Crott's Town, joined together and continued as one along a valley now called The Holler'.

The stream runs today as it did then, passing near Sugar Loaf Mountain and the village of Lambsburg, Virginia. As it continues southeast, more rivers and streams join in and it increases in size until it becomes an ocean, three hundred miles away in the sunrise.

Ten thousand years ago, the Indians came "from where the sun sleeps" and found a river in the shadow of a mountain. They built bark houses in the coves and valleys, raised families, hunted, fished and stored food for winter. They thanked the Gods for all blessings and all things and took only what was needed for survival. No one owned the land, the sky, or the river; everything belonged to the Higher Powers that caused it to be.

As the years passed, experience became their history and by word of mouth, they passed the knowledge down to the young. All were taught to respect and revere their elders, to tread lightly on the land and give thanks for all seasons and for all things. If they lived wisely, their time in the land would be long and someday they would join their ancestors, whose campfires could be seen burning in the nighttime sky; who were on a journey to a Great Hunting Ground somewhere beyond the sun.

Then came rumors of strange people with white faces, who came from the Great Water in huge canoes driven by the wind; who wore strange clothing, spoke a strange language and carried dreadful sticks that spoke with thunder and killed with magic.

Ancient legends told of a time when a Great White God would come from the Great Water, a God with terrible powers who would own the land, the people and the animals. He would smite all who kept to the old ways and the Earth as they knew it, would be no more. And so it became.

By wagon, horseback and on foot the settlers came, from "Down East" along the Great Wagon Road. All came with dreams of freedom and a brand new life in a brand new land. They would clear the land, build homes, raise families, pay no taxes, worship when, where and if they pleased and be beholden to no man.

Some few found a river in the shadow of Sugar Loaf Mountain and called it home. The Indians were already gone and for the first time ever, someone now owned the land, the river and the sky. They chopped fields from the forest with hand-tools, built log cabin homes on the new frontier, hunted, fished and stored food for winter. As the Indians had done before them, they believed if they worked hard and lived a good life, their time in the land would be long and when they died, they would go to heaven somewhere up there beyond the sun.

All came with a basic knowledge of farming, but in a land so new and strange, there were many unknowns; some were life threatening and came without warning. Summers brought droughts, thunderstorms, hail and floods and winters brought snow, ice, blizzards and a freezing wind that blew for weeks on end.

Three other seasons were given to prepare for the worst one: planting, hoeing, harvesting and storing food. They learned when, where, what, how to plant, when to harvest and how to stay alive in the hot fields of summer. Some days tried their souls, but even the worst came to an end, bringing a night of rest so they could do it all over again tomorrow. When winter came roaring down from the mountain, they were ready and with food, shelter and a little luck, they just might live to see spring come again.

Winters were long, hard and life threatening and during the worst blizzards, they had no choice but to stay inside by the roaring fireplace. With food, shelter and firewood, they were safe unless the house burned down. Someday they would tell their grandchildren, "It was a little rough back there in the Good Old Days."

The coming of spring brought a renewal of faith throughout the land and every farmer knew deep in his soul it would be a good crop year. "They aint no use in plantin' no seeds if you ain't got no faith." Hope was eternal in the fields of spring and if the rains came, it would be the best year ever: with "corn stalks so big, we'll have to saw 'em down with a crosscut saw, split 'em up with the ax and haul 'em home like stove wood."

As the years passed and their knowledge increased, they learned to make a living in the good years and the bad. They knew when rain was coming and how much snow was coming in winter and passed the knowledge down to the young.

Homes were far between in the early years and people felt crowded if they could see smoke from a neighbor's chimney. Even in the 1930s, our next-door neighbors were almost a mile away, but we could hear them chopping wood, their dogs barking, their rooster crowing and smell smoke from their chimney.

Most homes were built in a valley beside a "good year-round spring" and every family had "the best water God ever made." As late as the 1940s, those who continued using springs, continued to brag about their water, "We got the best spring you ever seen in this whole country."

Some few people "wern't about to be hemmed up down yonder in no holler" and built their homes on high ridges, far from a water source. From the top of the world, they could look down on the neighbors and see the thunderstorms of summer and the snows of winter come over the mountain. The views were terrific and they could see forever, but they learned to live with much less water than their neighbors.

That was the story at our house, because Pa didn't think like ordinary people. We lived on a high dry ridge, with "the best spring water God ever made, way down yonder in the holler' at the bottom of the hill." Through the years, we carried enough of it uphill to float half the county.

As time passed, wells replaced springs and well water became "the best water in the whole country." We continued using the spring until about 1940, when we became the owners of a brand new hand-dug well, just before my legs wore off at the knees. It was like moving to town and we immediately had the best well water "God ever made" just outside the kitchen door.

Most who came to the area lived out their lives digging a living from the Earth. From early spring until late fall, they lived in the fields, but when winter came, they were prepared for the frightening events that came over the Blue Ridge Mountain. They came every winter: in the form of blizzards, deep snow, sleet, freezing rain and the cold un-ending wind that drove people mad. Fireplaces warmed them by day, heavy quilts warmed them by night and by faith, hope, "damnation and plain ol' cussedness," they survived, sometimes barely, until spring.

Almost all were one-horse (sometimes no-horse) farmers who lived simply and close to the land. To a family, they planted gardens and cornfields and with horses, mules and manpower, dug a living from the top few inches of the Earth.

Neighbors were real neighbors, who shared trials and tribulations and helped each other in times of need. House raisings, barn raisings, corn shuckings and new-ground clearings were among the hardest jobs and all were easier when shared. The gatherings also gave them a chance to socialize and break the grinding everyday routine of life on the farm.

As the years passed, the river became home and its name became Stewart's Creek. The area prospered as new generations of children and grandchildren plowed the earth and sowed the seeds. As they grew up, they too lived as their parents and grandparents had done before them and became one-horse farmers, often in the same fields.

Some few of the early people are buried in a small cemetery beside the Graveyard Road, on a hilltop high above Stewart's Creek. There are no names or dates on the sand-rock headstones and tall trees have grown up among the graves. Following tradition, the people were buried with their heads to the west, assuring that the sun will shine in their faces when they rise up on Resurrection Morning.

The first of my ancestors in the new world (Michael Easter) came from Holland in the 1700s and settled in Davidson/Rowan County, North Carolina. He became sick in 1783 and made a will that described how he wanted his property divided.

In 1827, David Easter moved from Davidson County to Carroll County, Virginia and settled in the shadow of Sugar Loaf Mountain. He became the first of my many kin people in that area and his eight sons served in the Civil War. All returned home except Daniel, who died of pneumonia in a Maryland prison camp.

In 1901, my grandparents, George Washington Easter and Alice Berrier Easter bought a tract of land in Surry County, North Carolina and moved there from the Flower Gap area of Carroll County. They built a one-room log cabin in a wooded valley a half-mile west of Stewart's Creek, cleared new fields from the forest, built split-rail fences, tended the land and livestock, planted fruit trees and grape vines; raised a family and learned how to make a living. All of their neighbors said of them, "They're good people and they don't bother nobody."

My Dad, Kermit Easter, the fourth and youngest of their four children, was born November 17, 1909. My Mother, Elizabeth Whitaker Easter, one of Bob and Mollie Wood Whitaker's thirteen children, was born May 29, 1916. They were married February 27, 1931 in Hillsville, Virginia and set up housekeeping in what Mama called a shack near Pine Ridge.

They later moved to a one-room log cabin at the foot of Jim's Knob and having no money, no horse or cow, no plow or wagon, they depended heavily on my grandparents. Other than working on the Beamer Bridge on Highway 89 for a few days and "off bearing" lumber at sawmills, my dad (Pa) did no "outside work," as he called it. For the first few years, they barely eked out a living and as it was for Grandpa, farming was the only way of life.

The Hiatt House

The cabin stood on what Pa called, "The windiest damn ridge I ever seen." I was born there in 1932 and although we paid no rent, it was not a good place to live. Alfred Hiatt lived there in later years and it became known as the Hiatt House.

The white-oak shingles lay flat on the roof: proving they were made in the right moon sign and spaces between the logs were daubed with red mud. Large field rocks supported the four corners and there was no under-pinning. A rock and mud chimney stood on the west end, with a small four-pane window beside it.

Jim Smith's bob' wire fence was the only protection from the fierce winter winds that came "straight outta' Bobbitt Holler'," as Pa said it. Wind snow often covered the bedspread in winter and they swept more off the floor of the overhead loft before it melted and dripped downstairs.

Nobody liked living in the Hiatt House, including Roby and Sarah Smith who built it. The biggest problem was the spring, located "way down yonder in Walter Marshall's Woods." Jim Smith's spring was about the same distance away, as was his son Farley's in Hoot Owl Holler'. While we lived there, Mama placed the table leg on my gown to keep me out of the fireplace while she carried water from the spring. After about a year, we moved to Fred Marshall's house (The Fred House) on the south side of Jim's Knob. My brother Warren was born there December 24, 1934 and became Mama's "Christmas Youngun'."

We then moved to Oscar Marshall's "New House" in the valley near his brother Little Sid. My first memories are of living there, when thanks to Grandpa, Santa brought a Red Flyer wagon and a metal toy truck with real headlights powered by flashlight batteries.

I have a few other faint memories of pulling the wagon downhill to the barn with the truck on board, the kitchen, the stairway, the garden and a neighbor who came by: Lester "Butch" Faulkner. Being unable to pronounce his nickname, I called him "Bush."

Grandpa then gave us 20 acres of land and with the help of neighbors and a house raising, we became the owners of a brand new one-room log cabin on the same road as the Hiatt House. We continued sharecropping other's fields, but as a family, we never again lived in anyone else's house. It became our home, where my four brothers and I grew up cutting stove wood, hoeing corn and running wild in the woods.

Most of our time was spent doing the jobs that had to be done and done "right now, right this very minute." We never grew hay, but one of Pa's favorite sayings was, "Roll outta' that bed, boys, we gotta' make hay while the sun shines." We almost lived in the fields of summer: plowing, hoeing and harvesting and thanks to Pa, Mama and Mother Nature, we missed no meals. Anything we didn't can, dry or store, we ate, which was my favorite part.

We began so far down the economic ladder; our situation had to improve and began doing so when Pa bought a horse. He and I built a sourwood sled and for the first time ever; we had our own transportation. (I'd almost finished high school when he bought our first car: a well-used A-Model Howard Hawks of Lambsburg had used on his mail route.)

We carried so much water up the hill, the spring path wore deep and the more we carried, the shorter our legs became and the deeper the path. Grandpa and Grandma also had a deep spring path and they too had short legs. Our well probably came along at about right time, because the buckets were already dragging on the ground.

With mattock, shovel, manpower and sweat, Bud Crotts hand-dug our new well about 1940. We continued used the spring box for cooling milk and other foods, but never again did we carry water up the hill. For some reason, our short legs became semi-permanent and none of my family ever fully recovered.

With the coming of electricity, we brought a new refrigerator and no longer stored food in the spring box. For the first time ever, we had milk as cold as the Ed Smiths, who had electricity years earlier. We then had ice water and ice-cold lemonade, without waiting for Foot Washing Day at Crooked Oak Church.

We wound water from the well until the spring of 1955. I'd just got home from the army and while sleeping late on my day off; Mama chased me out of bed to wind up wash water. I bought a new well pump from Alec Marshall at Shelton Plumbing in Mt. Airy and my brother Warren and I dived in.

We 'ciphered, measured, dug ditches, sweated and thanks to some good advice from Alec and three twenty-five-mile round-trips to town, we got it all together. (We also had some good help from Pa, "You all gonna' 'lectrocute the whole damn family.") After some nineteen years, we had running water in the house and nobody cried about the end of winding water from the well.

Some of our older neighbors had never learned to read and had "no use for such doings." Their thinking, "It don't take much book learnin' to foller' a mule's rear end across them fields all day." (Anyone who wanted to learn depended on Sid Jarrell, a schoolteacher who walked all over our country in the 1930s, teaching people to read.)

When one-room schools came into being, most kids, including Pa and Mama, learned at least some of the Three R's. As *we* grew up, Mama told us, "You go to school and learn something or you gonna' grow up dumb." (I often wonder if it worked in my case.)

For the first dozen years, the best place to read at our house was beside the kerosene lamp. When we ran out of kerosene oil, we "went to bed with the chickens" and "got up when the rooster crowed." Nobody liked sitting in the dark when they could neither see nor read. When we got electricity, it was like moving to town and I could read anywhere in the house, on the darkest days: even at midnight.

An electric stove brought an end to sawing wood for the cook stove, a problem Warren and I had a terrible time adjusting to. "What on earth would we do with all that extra free time?" Mama no longer had to baby the wood cook stove and bake herself alive while cooking meals on hot summer days. Electricity may not have been the best thing that happened on our hill, but it came close and nobody complained until the power bill came.

The final edition of home

As my three younger brothers came into the world, more rooms were added to the one-room cabin. The first was a combination kitchen and bedroom on the back: "a shed" as Mama called it. We eventually had a four-room house, with a new kitchen, living room, an attic, a small bedroom on the front porch and a mudroom beside the kitchen.

The five boys, from the left: Warren, Big Mike, Curtis, El and Wayne (1950s)

My younger brothers were: Warren, born December 24, 1934, Curtis, born July 13, 1941, Eldridge (El), September 18, 1947 and Big Mike, March 5, 1950. As my three youngest brothers grew up, they too ran wild in the woods as Warren and I had done. With five boys running wide-open for so many years, our whole country got a terrific workout. Somehow, the Earth survived and most likely, none of us would've been any happier if we'd had lots of money and good sense.

Two show-offs at the home place in the 1940s: Wayne and Curtis

Two show-offs at the home place in the 1950s: Big Mike and El

Somewhere over yonder hill……..

Chapter 2

Exploring

The Great Outdoors

The worst place a famous scout and hunter could be was hemmed up in a schoolroom. Lunch, recess and art classes were o k, but with catfish jumping out on the bank down at the Abe Hole, it was just like being in jail. Worst of all, the mean-eyed teacher up front had a big paddle and was just waiting for me to mess up.

I was moping along in reading class one day, when a book about some talking chickens got my attention. Even *I* knew our chickens back home had never talked: at least not to me, but a light bulb flashed in my dark attic and some of the printed words began making sense. Reading was soon right up there with lunch, recess and girls and with hundreds of books in the school library I could check out, it was like living in the "Promised Land."

On cold winter nights, nothing existed, but the warm wood heater, the kerosene lamp, a book and me. Using other people's minds, I traveled to the ends of the Earth, the bottom of the ocean and the outer reaches of the universe.

Zane Grey and I rode horseback across the Great Western Plains and slept under the stars beside the Cimarron River. We herded the Devil's Cattle across a hundred miles of prairie scrub: (whatever that was) fighting outlaws and Indians all the way. Inspired by Street and Smith's Wild West Weekly Magazine, I built line shacks high in the mountains above Jim's Knob and watched sky-burning sunsets over the Arizona Desert.

One memorable night, Big Little Books and Dick Tracy took me on a whaling ship deep into the South Atlantic: chasing crooks in a snowstorm. I'd never before thought about snow falling on the ocean as it did on our mountains.

I searched for the lost continent of Atlantis deep under the ocean and mushed a dog team across frozen Arctic ice fields in a screaming blizzard. Just off the Horn of Africa, (wherever that was) I sent a dozen pirate ships to the Davy Jones Locker.

While reading by the attic window one rainy day, Buck Rogers and I headed for the stars in a spaceship shaped like a huge shiny stovepipe: with the top end sharpened like a pencil. We left Stewart's Creek far behind as we climbed higher and higher into the sky. We traveled faster than the speed of light, found the end of time far beyond something called *infinity* and came back home a hundred years before we started. My nighttime sky was forever changed, as I gained some small idea of how big and complicated the universe might be.

Thanks to a chuck wagon, my storybook cowboys had food to eat every day, which was great news, because no hero of mine should ever go hungry. One lucky cowboy camped far back in the mountains and boiled his coffee in a tin can. I could hardly wait to try it on my next mission into the Three Knobs.

After learning to read, our own fields and woods became a huge adventure land; Stewart's Creek became a wild raging river and our own Gardner Woods became the Great North Woods. I read about "gold in them thar' hills" and with three hills (knobs) standing in a row west of our house, my fortune was made. I could hardly wait to get there and start panning with one of Mama's pie pans.

I read about haints', werewolves, and other ungodly creatures that came out in full of the moon. I'd already been warned about some scary boogers out there in the witching hour, "Boy, them there woods is full a' things that'll scare your britches plumb off. Anybody got any sense a'tall, don't go prowlin' around out there in the dark, 'specially by his-self." (Just the thought of being lost in the woods at night scared my britches off.)

Double sundogs came up in the western sky: containing all the colors of a rainbow. Grandpa could study them, predict coming events and forecast the weather. With the whole world full of signs and omens, I decided to do some predicting and forecasting of my own. I might even become famous.

Thank my lucky stars I didn't tell anybody about it, because seeing an omen in a cloud formation and predicting what would happen tomorrow was a whole lot harder than I'd thought. Just because an ugly buzzard flew over didn't mean something bad would happen, even if I *didn't* like its looks. No matter what kind of omen showed up or what I tried to do about it, the world continued on its merry way. I finally figured out that people who could actually read signs understood everything in Blum's Almanac. No wonder I couldn't forecast anything.

Property lines and trespassing did not exist for young hunters and fishers in the wild hills of home. From Henry McCraw's bottoms in Virginia, to Dave Carson's bottoms "way down yonder in Carolina," Stewart's Creek was almost mine. I seldom saw anyone else while rambling along its banks, or anywhere else for that matter.

High adventure came easy in the laurel thickets and honeysuckle jungles along Stewart's Creek. I found hollow dead chestnut trees lying in the woods big enough to walk into, three-foot icicles hanging off the big rocks and strange animal dens. The Laurel Hells were tangled and almost impossible to climb through, which made them ideal for experienced scouts such as myself.

The house-sized boulders were hard to climb, dangerous when wet and icy, caused some very dirty clothes and some very choice words from Mama, "Where in the world you been wallerin' today? I wont never git them clothes clean again. If you don't stay outta' them bluffs, you ain't gonna' have nothing left fit to wear and you gonna' look funny runnin' around here nekkid as a jaybird."

Pa also had some good advice, "They aint nobody but a idiot climbs in them bluffs, boy. They's snakes in there bigger'n you are. You got any sense a'tall, you'll stay the (you know what) outta there." I never saw any snakes in the bluffs, but after a near disaster on ice-covered rocks, I found safer places to explore in winter.

According to legend, people once made wages panning for gold in the sandbars of Stewart Creek. With sandbars in every creek bend, there just had to be gold in some of them. I sneaked one of Mama's pie pans and panned and panned, but never found any. I did find dozens of old still places on backwoods streams, Indian arrowheads in the creek bottoms, wild animal tracks on the sandbars, deep dark fishing holes, black walnuts and wild strawberry fields. There was so much to see and do, no way could I ever get around to everything.

The bluff, seen from Grandpa's Bottom (1971)

The biggest bluff on Stewart's Creek began near Dave Carson's Big Bottom; continued by Grandpa's Bottom, (seen above) on by his house and ended in the Tom Hawks Woods far up the valley. From my lookout tree high in the bluff, I could see everywhere and best of all, nobody could see me. With rifle and telescope, I stayed ready to fight off an army, but no army ever showed up. The only things going were some crows chasing a hawk and buzzards floating around high overhead: hunting something dead, or maybe waiting for me to shoot something.

Over uncountable years, uncountable floods had piled uncountable rocks of uncountable colors and sizes along the creek. They varied in size from head-high boulders an ocean of water couldn't move, all the way down to small flat ones that skipped on top of the water when thrown just right. Best of all were the basket-ball-sized "chunkers" I could hardly lift, which made a big "chunk" sound when thrown in the creek.

Long sections of the creek idled along, then fed into roaring splashing rapids and deep dark fishing holes. There were so many sandbars it would take a lifetime to pan all of them for gold and with a whole lifetime ahead, I planned to do just that, some day.

There were enough great things right in our own back yard to keep me busy for a year, then I was "off to see the world." From what I'd read, there were castaways on the beaches of faraway islands who didn't have to hoe corn and tobacco in hot summer fields; all they had to do for breakfast was climb a coconut tree, then spend the rest of the day hunting, fishing and exploring.

I found old sawmill roads, animal trails and people-paths everywhere in the woods and all needed exploring. Come fair weather or foul, the great hunter on the prowl. Armed with .22 rifle, pocket knife and slingshot, I climbed through a hundred hillsides, searching for long gone bears and bad guys, but never found any.

I'd read that an ace scout, even with no flashlight or lantern, could track a black bear across a bare rock at midnight. He could tell how long it had been gone, how much it weighed, where it was headed and what it had for supper last night. I kept a sharp eye out but never saw the first bear track, not even in the sandbars. "How in the world could anybody learn anything about bear tracking with no bear tracks to track?"

Somebody once carved two bear paws from foot-long pieces of plank and drove nails in them for claws. He tied the paws on his shoes, walked through a ploughed field to make a huge set of bear tracks. Looking back on his handiwork, somehow it didn't look right and after some ciphering, considering and pondering, he realized bears had four feet, so to make two sets of tracks, he made another trip through the field.

A terrible malady called "Bear Mania" soon spread throughout the land, "You-all better look out, folks; they's a monster bear out yonder. Did you go see the size a' them tracks? Biggest I ever seen. If that thing comes this a' way, I'm a' headin' for the hills, 'cause I ain't got nothin' big enough to shoot it. Young-uns', you all stay outta' them woods, cause a bear that big eats people alive. Lordy mercy, what's gonna' happen to us next?"

Anyone planning a scouting mission into the backcountry needed to know survival tactics in case they got delayed or lost. Wild foods were sometimes scarce and after a couple of deep woods disasters; I learned that suppertime could come a little late.

I'd been warned, "They's stuff out there that'll put you in the Zion Hill Graveyard" and for that reason alone, I had a need-to-know which wild stuff was safe to eat. With hunger for a teacher, the Boy Scout motto became mine. With single-shot rifle, telescope, Barlow knife and a pocket full of Mama's corn bread, I was prepared. Even on the coldest, darkest days of January, nobody would go hungry in my country unless Mama ran out of corn bread.

With springs in almost every valley, nobody died of thirst in our world. A long-handled gourd or tin can was found at most springs; otherwise people drank directly from the water by lying on their stomachs, or rolled up a laurel leaf to dip up small amounts. (Grandpa, Pa and I drank water from laurel leaves at a dozen different springs.)

I drank from Stewart's Creek on occasion, with absolutely no doubt about its purity. It was a known fact that water flowing over rocks and sand purified it. Somebody said it was in the Bible and somebody else read it in the newspaper, so how much more proof did anybody need? Who ever heard of anybody dying from drinking creek water anyway?

While prospecting for gold one summer day, I followed a spring branch all the way down to Stewart's Creek. While cooling in the shade, I launched a dozen laurel-leaf boats on down-river-journeys to someday reach the ocean. They sailed out of sight around the bend and I've always wondered if they got there.

The moon was one big puzzle: it constantly changed in size, shape and brightness and where it was in the sky. It was huge on the horizon and smaller when overhead. It came up over the cowshed in summer and never climbed higher than the South-Forty treetops. In mid-winter, it came up over the granary and passed straight overhead. I never knew where it would come up next and sometimes it didn't come up at all.

The sun did the exact opposite: it stayed low in the southern sky in winter, but passed straight overhead in summer and cooked our brains. To complicate things even worse, the sun and the moon were sometimes in the sky at the same time and no way could anybody figure out what was going on.

Blum's Almanac was the farmer's Bible and had the answers to everything for anyone smart enough to figure it out. Sometimes the signs were in the head, sometimes in the feet and sometimes all over the place and I never knew which part of me would be next. It told the best days to fish: the blacker the little fish shapes for each day, the better the fish would bite. I already knew catfish bit better when the creek was muddy or at night, but figured it might be good to know about other days. As time went on, I learned that surviving in the wilderness required knowing a whole bunch of stuff about a whole bunch of stuff I knew nothing about.

Grandpa and Grandma followed the moon signs and kept the latest copy of the Blum's Almanac handy on the kitchen wall. They told a certain grandson, "If you wanta' grow a good garden, boy, you better learn them Zodiac signs. You plant just any old time, you might as well throw them seeds out to the chickens and save all that work." (My first garden was a six-foot by six-foot space beside the tobacco field and the signs must've been right, because the few hills of beans grew just fine.)

Our son Mike at the rainy-day shelter (February 1971)

An overhanging rock in Oscar Marshall's bluff was a great rainy-day shelter. It was as big as a house and somebody had built a campfire under it a long time ago. Maybe Daniel Boone camped there and never told anybody, or maybe it was the Indians.

I thought about camping there overnight, but never quite got around to it. Not that I was afraid or anything, but with all the laurel thickets, honeysuckle jungles and blackberry briars in the way, it would've been a long dangerous run back home in the dark. I'd already heard some terrible crashing noises in the woods at night and no way was I about to camp anywhere except in the daytime. I also didn't build any campfires under the rock, because Pa had told me in no uncertain terms, "You set them woods a' fire, boy and I'll set *your* woods a' fire." (All of my campfires were built on sandbars with plenty of creek-water handy.)

Daytime was a whole different story and every path and stream led to great wonders. What caused a ten-foot sinkhole in a may-apple field at the Curve Hole? What ripped a huge chestnut log completely apart in the Second Knob? Who piled up rocks under a tree in the middle of the Gardner Woods and when and what for? Where did all the arrowheads come from I found piled up beside an old stump in the Bob Faulkner Woods? As I got older, the questions kept coming and the list got longer.

When Linc Gardner died in 1935, nobody lived on his farm for many years and his huge Gardner Woods became one of my favorite places to ramble. While exploring a pathway on Gardner's Ridge, I was using every bit of my know-how in reading signs: trying to figure out who and what had been there before me.

I'd read that in order to sneak up on anything, you had to go quietly or "anything" would be long gone before you got there. With rifle at ready and eyes wide open, I was going quietly along the path when a pheasant flew up almost in my face. I was an "instant goner" and my hair headed for the hills, just like I almost did. (Even first-rate scouts like me sometimes got surprised.) Long after my heart quit racing, I thought about shooting at it: at least shooting the way it went.

Everybody talked about a place called the Tom Hawks Field. Nobody knew exactly where it was, but it was somewhere in the Tom Hawks Woods: just west of the Gardner Woods. I could already see the headlines, "Famous Stewart's Creek scout finds long-lost Tom Hawks Field."

In the early years, Grandpa hunted wild turkeys in the Tom Hawks Woods, but they were long gone by my time, just like the bears and deer. Except for pheasants beating their wings on dead logs and somebody running a still, not much happened in that part of the world.

On Mission D-Day, I gathered Remington single-shot, bolt-action .22 rifle, compass, a pocket full of corn bread and headed for the Tom Hawks Woods. I mushed new snow up the left valley above Grandpa's house and kept a sharp eye out, because trouble lurked everywhere in the backwoods. The trees were small and scrubby until I got into the Tom Hawks Woods, where they were older and larger and if a sawmill had ever been there, it had been a very long time.

I tramped all over "you know where and half a' Georgia" as Pa said it and found an old still place, a spring and animal tracks in the snow, but no Tom Hawks Field. How could that be? It had to be in there somewhere because everybody said it was. Somebody named Tom Hawks once cleared out a cornfield in the middle of nowhere, but where in tarnation was it? If I hadn't already known everything about everything, I might've asked a few questions. Only problem with that: experienced scouts did *not* go around showing people how dumb they were by asking questions.

By the end of the day, I knew no more than I'd known going in, night was coming, the corn bread was gone and I was cold and starving. Even being a tough outdoorsman who could go without food for an hour, just thinking about Mama cooking supper in a warm house brought an end to another great mission. Once again, I could see the headlines: "Experienced scout fails Tom Hawks Mission."

I later hewed out my very own mile-long Tom Hawks Trail from our house to Mail Box Hill. Talk about blazing a new trail through un-scouted territory? Daniel Boone could've done no better. Here was a modern-day pathfinder and seeker of far places keeping an eye out for the unknown, chopping his way to fame and glory in the Great North Woods with the best of equipment: Pa's *good* axe. (I hoped and prayed he never found out about it.)

My trail led downhill by the cowshed, continued by the watering hole and angled up across a wooded hillside to a ridge in our South-Forty Woods. It continued downhill to a spring branch that began at the "Fred House" on Jim's Knob.

After a break in the shade, I tackled the worst place of all, a north-facing laurel thicket beyond the branch. Laurel thickets were hard to climb through, let alone chop a path through, but in any case, destiny called and a long while later, a worn-out me came out into Grandpa's worn-out field east of Walter Marshall's house.

The going was easier in the field of sassafras and locust bushes, but got harder again in the woods beyond. Like all good scouts, I blazed trees to mark my trail and eventually came out on Lambsburg Road at the foot of Mailbox Hill. A brand new trail now bypassed the Big Curve and if anybody ever found the Tom Hawks Field, we would both be famous.

Jim's Knob was our nearest high country and from Jim's hillside field, I could see everywhere. The Walter and Fred Marshall houses were laid out far down to the south and the Tom Hawks Woods stretched out all over creation at the right front. Straight down in front stood the Hiatt House, our house and Grandpa's house and beyond Stewart's Creek was Cleve Thomas's fields.

Some big white pines marked the Graveyard Road and Houston Thomas's white house stood on the hilltop beyond. Far away to the north was the Porter Hawks house on Piper's Gap Road and at far left was the village of Lambsburg at the foot of Sugar Loaf Mountain.

When leaves changed color in October, I could spot hickory trees from the knob, which were the darkest yellow of all. (Hungry squirrel hunters needed to know where they were when squirrels began eating hickory nuts in late summer.)

I watched late day storms push ice-cream-colored thunderheads into the eastern sky, as lightning flashed weakly: too far away to hear the thunder. I daydreamed of flying up there among them in my own yellow Piper Cub. It could happen, because my landing field was already waiting at the bottom of the knob: Jim Smith's peanut field. (The fact that the field was too short for a runway didn't matter; it would still be my landing field.)

Pilot Mountain, seen from Jim's Knob (November 2007)

    I could see Mt. Airy twelve miles away to the east and twenty-some miles away stood Pilot Mountain. (Seen above.) A huge wall of mountains climbed into the sky behind the knob and continued northeast as far as the eye could see: finally fading into the mist, somewhere in Virginia.

    Fisher's Peak was the tallest of all and promised mystery, adventure and a huge challenge for anyone brave enough to climb it. As I learned the hard way, it was very steep, very tall and very hard to climb. Pa's generation was tougher than mine, because they routinely climbed the mountain and held Sunday picnics on Bald Rock.

    I telescoped Bald Rock and all of the snowy mountainsides, hoping to spot the wild goats said to be there. I kept an eye out for Japanese Zeroes making a bombing run on Gardner's Ridge, wore out the nighttime sky, found the Man in the Moon and tried to sort out the Milky Way.

The fire tower on Fisher's Peak (1948)

    A fire tower was built on Fisher's Peak in 1948 and we rode there one Sunday with the John Hawks family. Just before we got to the tower, the universal joint broke in their 1936 Chevrolet. John said he needed a fertilizer sack full of parts to go anywhere but forgot to bring the sack along that day. We walked on to the tower and I made the above photo: one of my first with my first roll of film.

From high in the tower, God's country was laid out like a map down below. Round Peak was straight down to the right; Lambsburg and Sugar Loaf Mountain stood far to the left and Jim's Knob, the other two knobs, our house and Grandpa's house were straight down in front. It was like being on top of the world and there was so much to see, I could've stayed all day.

All too soon, a thunderstorm brought our sightseeing to an end. The thunder was loud and frightening and we took shelter in the car. Someone from Lambsburg gave us a ride home and John went back next day and replaced the universal joint.

The fire tower was there for many years, but we only made the one trip to see it. When towers fell out of favor, it was dismantled and an F M radio tower was built on the same spot. Fisher's Peak was never again as impressive as it was with a tall tower standing on top: protecting the world from forest fires.

(While checking the mountainside with binoculars some years later, I saw a building about halfway up Fisher's Peak. Mike Edwards later told me his family once owned a herd of goats that ran free in the mountain and the building was their shelter. When all Carroll County, Virginia roads were named, the Edwards Road became Goat House Road.)

January Winter

One day in January winter, Jack London and I took a break from chasing outlaws and built a campfire on a Stewart's Creek sandbar. We boiled coffee in a tin can of creek water, found black walnuts under a tree and they became a feast when eaten with Mama's cornbread. (So much for people who said you couldn't survive in the wilderness.) All the while, my trusty rifle stayed handy, because danger lurked behind every tree and you had to be ready for anything at any time.

As we rested and warmed, wind snow began blowing from straight off Sugar Loaf Mountain. It rode the wind sideways and stuck on the north side of trees. The whole world slowly turned white and we almost had ourselves a blizzard. Imagination threw me headfirst into the Great North Woods I'd read about and Stewart's Creek became a wild raging river. I could almost see the Northern Lights flickering overhead and hear wolves howling toward Dave Carson's bottoms.

As the campfire died down, another great expedition came to an end and I headed home along a pathway that was fast becoming white. We'd get them outlaws tomorrow, but right now, supper was waiting in a warm home just over yonder hill.

After every snowfall, the great wilderness called the great explorer and I could hardly wait to head for the hills. Every path in the woods was brand new, because no one had been there in the new snow. With rifle, telescope and Pa's knee-length rubber boots, I waded deep into the backwoods: "roughing it" just like my storybook heroes in the Great North Woods. No one knew where I was, because secret missions were supposed to be just that: a secret. Places to explore were endless and there was always something new waiting just over the next hill and it would take forever to get around and see it all.

    Sadly, the days were never long enough, especially in winter. Sundown came early and falling temperatures once again brought visions of a warm heater waiting back home and I could almost taste the supper Mama was cooking. My storybook heroes sometimes slept all night in the snow, but me? I headed for home.

In Jim's Knob (2002)

Foot-log to nowhere

Dreamland

Chapter 3
Daydreams

Birds could just flap their wings and take to the sky and it looked so easy, I wondered why people couldn't do that. Figuring nobody had tried hard enough, I took a bundle of fodder in each hand and flapped as hard and as fast as I could, but never got off the ground. Somebody tried flying from the barn roof with two bundles of fodder and "got all stoved up." "Boy, you'd a' been meant to fly, they'd a' put wings on you."

Two brothers, Orville and Wilber Easter made kites from broom straw stems and newspapers that either crashed on takeoff or landed in a tree. We whittled out wooden windmills that became airplane propellers and the faster *we* ran, the faster *they* ran, but we never got off the ground.

I was climbing a tall 'possum pine one day, when the wind almost blew me away. As the tree swayed wildly back and forth, I hung on for dear life and had another silent conversation with my Maker, "Just let me get back on the ground, Lord and I'll never do it again." (I didn't climb anymore 'possum pines.)

With airplanes on the brain, my heart and soul flew with the twin engine DC 3s as they lumbered across our Blue Ridge sky. Albert Eades came over in a yellow Piper Cub, "Hauling peanuts to Galax," according to Pa. "Now there was a lucky man, flying way up there and eating peanuts too." A "twin tail" P-38 came over Grandpa's place: going so fast I almost missed it. "How in the world could anything go that fast?" I'd have traded everything I owned for a ride and maybe stuff I'd own later.

During the Big War, formations of military planes came over, with some pulling gliders. I'd studied the silhouettes that came in the newspapers and knew the shapes of all war planes. I kept an eye on the sky at all times, just in case a Japanese Zero came by. Mama said, "You go around with your head up in the air all the time." Her wise son (who at that time knew everything) replied, "What do you expect me to do, go around with it in the ground?"

I dreamed of fighters and bombers flying high overhead: searching for something important. If I'd had a set of wings, I'd have been up there helping them find whatever they were looking for. I had recurring dreams of an airplane falling out of the sky directly down on me. I was unable to move, but always woke up just in the nick of time, scared half to death; with my heart racing wide open.

The inside wall of most log homes were covered with magazine and newspaper pages: glued there with flour paste to keep out the winter wind. They were like a library and I read stories of war, famine in the land and strange exciting far away places.

A story on Farley Smith's wall told of a pilot, an airplane and a dog named Tailskid. The story never got old and I read it every time I went by. He and Tailskid flew into the thunderclouds in their shiny red plane and from high in the sky, they could see the tiny roads and houses far below on the green Earth.

Anybody that lucky had to have a whole sack of buckeyes and rabbit's feet and no telling what else. I'd have traded all of my worldly goods for just one ride; I could always get another rifle, Barlow knife and telescope. Why couldn't I be his dog for a day?

A Progressive Farmer magazine came in Grandpa's mail, with a front-page photo of the plane of my dreams: a yellow Piper Cub just like the one Albert Eades flew. It was hard to imagine a farmer rich enough to own an airplane, not to mention a green pasture level enough for it to land in. We only had a horse and a cow in ours, it was on a hillside with very little grass and it was usually brown. (In the middle of summer, we often had no grass at all.)

My fighter plane from the 1940s

With scrap lumber from a sawmill place, Mama's butcher knife and my trusty Barlow, I whittled out some semblance of a WW2 fighter plane. (Seen above.) With so many other projects in the wind, it never got off the ground. Even so, an untold number of German and Japanese fighters went down in flames as I whittled along. (In 1977, my brother El found my plane in the attic of our old house. It was then over 30 years old and is now over 70 and to this day, it hangs in the ceiling of my basement, still standing watch for Japanese Zeroes.)

On a weekend in the early 1950s, some young men of the world were riding around in my first car, trying to impress everybody and look important. We were loafing at an Esso service station on West Lebanon Street in Mount Airy, when a formation of military fighter planes flew over. I was still "all eat-up" with airplanes and watched until they were almost out of sight.

When far down the country, one of the planes dropped out of formation, began spinning around and went down below the horizon. I'd had so many dreams of planes falling out of the sky; it was like one of them coming true. We later heard a plane had crashed near Westfield, drove there and found a huge smoking hole in the ground. The pilot had bailed out with a parachute, was o k and I felt strangely relieved the plane hadn't fallen on me.

During the Big War, I dreamed a huge gray Navy battleship had dropped anchor in Stewart's Creek at Oscar Marshall's bottoms. It was as tall as the surrounding hills and I remember thinking somebody had done a great job bringing it that far from the ocean. (When Watershed Lake was built there in the 1970s, there was enough water to float it.)

Everybody daydreamed of fantastic faraway places: New York, Chicago, Memphis, Down East, East Virginia, West Virginia, Down in Georgia, Out West and others: all described in glowing terms. Pa talked about Nashville, Wheeling West Virginia and WJJD Chicago, but he never got there. He also liked the Wild West and had he been born sooner, he'd have gone west with the wagons in '49.

He told of a neighbor, Ellis Thomas, who tried to fly by jumping into every whirlwind (dust devil) he saw. He "turned up missing" one day and was never heard of again. I wondered if a whirlwind picked him up and carried him far away.

Pa's older brother Manuel got his first job in Galax and later became a sheepherder in Oregon. He moved back to Galax, got married and owned a restaurant for several years. He, his wife Kate, son Kenneth and daughter Delores then moved to Oregon and never moved back. He was the only one of the four kids in his family who moved out of Surry County.

While climbing a snowy hillside one winter day, I heard the steam train whistle 12 miles away in Mt. Airy. I'd heard it before when the air was just right, but that day, it sent me a message loud and clear, "Come ride and we'll find the winter home of summer far away south. We'll blow that whistle long and loud at every railroad crossing between here and Georgia: telling one and all to get out of the way; that we're on an important mission. Somewhere down there we'll find spring, thaw our cold feet in a warm ocean and daydream about the winter we left behind."

"We'll find New York, Chicago and Memphis and like Uncle Manuel, find another ocean way out west. As our neighbors did in the 1920s, we'll ride the train north into the coalfields of West Virginia, dig that coal, bring home a barrel of money and never have to work again. With all that money, we'll hire somebody to plow the land, sow the seeds, cut the firewood and keep the home fires burning, while we spend eternity prowling all the rivers in the whole world."

Three knobs stood in a row just west of our house and I never grew tired of rambling the hillsides. Nettle's Knob was closest and my favorite. Since Jim Smith's field was on the side of it, we named it "Jim's Knob." (Frank's Knob would've been a better name, because Frank Coalson owned the land on top.)

While working in Jim's field, we rested on a hickory tree a tornado had blown down some years earlier. It was a corner property marker for the lands of Jim Smith, Walter Marshall and Frank Coalson. I had a vivid dream of sitting on the fallen tree and watching a tornado rip through the Tom Hawk's Woods down below. The air was full of flying limbs and trees, along with a black bear that was spun around a few times and thrown back to the ground. It was a scary dream that worried me for a very long time.

Historical information sign located on Highway 89 at Pine Ridge

Hardin "Skitt" Taliaferro mentioned Nettle's Knob in his book "Fisher's River Scenes." (Published in 1859.) With tongue in cheek, he wrote about the people he grew up with in the 1820s in the Little Fish River and Stewart's Creek areas. Almost all were hard working souls who lived even closer to the land than my family. (After a few days of hoeing corn in the hot summer sun, I wondered if that was even possible.)

"Skitt" wrote about simple people who hunted, fished and dug a living from the rocky hillsides: just as my family would be doing 120 years later. They also kept homemade spirits on hand for snakebites and other medicinal emergencies: just like us. They called it "Knock-'em-Stiff" and it proved to be powerful stuff, because many of their descendants still live in our area today.

Walter Marshall's apple orchard was on a steep hillside beside Jim's field and when apples fell off the trees, they rolled all the way to the bottom of the knob. "Just be down there with a fertilize' sack, boy, and catch 'em as they come bouncin' down the hill."

I made my first trip to the top of Jim's Knob around 1940 and found a fallen chestnut tree lying in the woods big enough to walk into. (It was still there some twenty years later when Helen and I bought the land. In 2004, I found the remains of another smaller one on the western slope: it had been dead for 70 or more years.)

In the foreground: Jim's Knob: with the Second Knob at center: the Third Knob at the extreme far left and in the far right background: Fisher's Peak. (1960s)

I sat under an apple tree in Jim's field and daydreamed about far-away places. Somewhere out there was a place called Paradise, where people rode airplanes, trains, automobiles and magic carpets; where you lived forever and the streets were paved with gold: a land of milk and honey, where you became rich and famous and built your parents a new house.

I searched for El Dorado's lost gold mine in a South American jungle and the lost city of Atlantis on the bottom of the ocean. I dug pirate treasures from the sands of South Sea Islands and with my yellow Piper Cub to take me there, nowhere on earth was safe from daydreams and some day I'd get there and see it all. As the sun went down behind Fisher's Peak, I returned to my landing field. (Jim Smith's peanut field beside the Big Mud Hole.) Tomorrow was coming in the morning and my yellow Piper Cub and I would be ready and raring to go.

By late August, last winter's fatback had become old and stale and everybody craved a "mess" of fresh meat. Squirrels began eating hickory nuts about that time and everybody I knew went squirrel hunting. Shotguns then boomed all over the country, sounding like a war had begun.

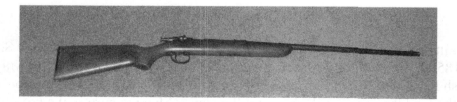

My best pal

Owning a shotgun or rifle was a rite of passage for young scouts and hunters and I eventually became the proud owner of a used Remington single-shot .22. (Seen above.) Some good advice came with the rifle, "Boy, don't you go pointin' that thing at nothin' you ain't gonna' shoot."

My first great squirrel hunt took place in Jim's Knob. While sneaking up the hillside, I saw one eating a hickory nut and got so excited I had to lean against another tree to hold the rifle still enough to shoot. I gently pulled the trigger like everybody said to do and it was a total surprise when the squirrel fell to the ground. I ran all the way home to show Mama. Bringing food home to help feed my family was special and next day's breakfast was even more special. Like all good gunslingers, I cut a notch on the rifle stock to record my first squirrel.

A swayback ridge connected Jim's Knob and the Second Knob, which Pa called "Dault Knob" and others called Moore's Fork Knob. There was no path or road between the two, but in later years, a sawmill road ran along the ridge. There were more dead chestnut trees lying in the Second Knob, but none as big as the one on Jim's Knob.

Grapevines grew in the hillside trees and when Tarzan went swinging, he hung onto the vines for dear life, because the landing place was far away at the bottom of the hill. Hurley Smith hunted squirrels in the Second Knob, but it was not my favorite place. When I shot one out of a tree, it fell downhill forever and it was no fun going to the bottom of the knob to find it.

The Second knob (at right) from Lambsburg/Pine Ridge Road (1971)

When dogwood trees bloomed in spring, the Second Knob hillside became a sea of white and when poplars changed color in fall, it became a sea of yellow. When the leaves fell in fall of the year, they were blown from the ridges into the deep hollows, becoming waist deep and hard to wade through. They gradually decayed and fed the huge poplars that grew there. I panned for gold in the Second Knob, but never found the first flake. I did find twenty some arrowheads piled up beside an old stump, which was almost as good. It also brought more questions to add to the many I already had about everything.

One cold winter day, I mushed six inches of snow across the top of all three knobs. From the top of the Third Knob, I watched smoke climb into the sky from the houses far down in Round Peak. (It was comforting to know there were still warm people somewhere in the world.)

Dogs were running something in the valley and I heard a woodcutter chopping wood toward Fisher's Peak. A car was spinning in the snow toward Lambsburg and Walter Marshall's gasoline powered washing machine "putt putted" back at the foot of Jim's Knob. Black crows sat in the bare tree limbs and a hungry cow bawled somewhere. Sugar Loaf Mountain stood frozen over Lambsburg and the mountains continued forever along the skyline. I was a very cold King of all I could see from the top of the world and a long way from home in the deep snow.

After wading so far in the snow that day, I never again climbed to the top of the Third Knob, but made other trips into the lower slopes. One-legged Big Sid Marshall once lived in one of the hollows, but all that remained were a few chimney rocks and the redbud trees and daffodils that still bloomed in spring; everything else had gone back to the forest.

The Third knob (Seen from Virginia.)

Bald Rock on Fisher's Peak (2009)

When seen from the top of any of the three knobs, Fisher's Peak filled the whole western sky: with Bald Rock sitting on top. (On an October weekend in 1975, we made a home movie of hang gliders as they launched from the rock. They sailed around in the air for a very long time and then landed in a pasture in Round Peak. As exciting as it was to see somebody jump off a mountain, it was far down my list of things to do. The city of Galax owned the mountaintop and eventually stopped the hang gliders due to liability issues.)

I never found gold in the Three Knobs or anywhere else for that matter, but thanks to Willard Lindsay, I figured it was just a matter of time. He lived between the Three Knobs and Fisher's Peak and was the luckiest person I knew; a buckeye tree grew at his house and he didn't care how many I got.

By carrying a buckeye in your pocket and holding your mouth just right, good luck would come your way as sure as shootin'. Every kid I knew carried one and I sometimes carried two, because luck was something you could never have too much of. I was told, "Them things is pizen, boy. You eat one of them things, you gonna' run outta' good luck and you gonna' think you done died and you just might."

Part 2

Winter pasture on the Holly Grove/Casper Stewart Road (1970s)

The Road to Home

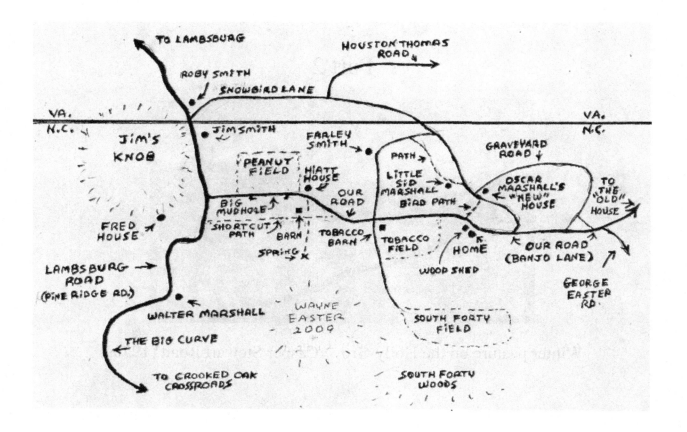

Chapter 4

The Road to Home

Our main public road was a muddy nightmare in winter and anyone who drove on it needed to take their dinner along, because it might be a while before they got back home. Every car that came by was the same color: the color of mud and when a clean one came along, it too was soon stuck in the mud on Lambsburg Road.

When at its worst, local men gathered drag pans, shovels, horses, mules and mattocks and tried to repair the worst places. No matter how hard they tried, Lambsburg Road remained "the worst road in the country" until it was paved.

Our road, (Banjo Lane) seen from Lambsburg Road (2009)

"Our road" branched east off Lambsburg Road at foot of Jim's Knob and had no name: we called it simply "Our Road." We lived a half-mile down the hill in what began as a one-room log cabin my parents built in 1936. Most of our road traffic was sleds, wagons, horseback riders, people on foot and maybe a stray cow or a dog. Seeing a car come down our hill was almost as exciting as seeing an airplane fly over. (When all county roads were was named in the 1990s, our road became Banjo Lane.)

Jim Smith's "bob-wire" pasture fence cornered at the intersection of our road and Lambsburg Road. His low-slung cowshed was just like my grandfather's: made of poles, covered with rough planks and almost tall enough for the cow to get into. His two-room log house, vineyard and log wine barn stood beyond the pasture and across the valley, a road led over a hill to the Houston Thomas home on Stewart's Creek. Still farther in the background stood Sugar Loaf Mountain at Lambsburg.

Our road ran downhill from the Lambsburg Road and with a "good running start," my bicycle would coast all the way home. By pumping the pedals a few times and holding my mouth just right, I could coast all the way to Oscar Marshall's Old House on Stewart's Creek. I tried hard to "pull it" back up the hill, but like most cycling in our hill country, it was "more push than ride." Apparently, the old folks had it even worse back in their day, "It was up-hill ever' which-a-way we went, goin' and 'a comin' back too and we didn't have no bicycle like you boys and we got wore to a nub.")

Nobody worried much about keeping our road repaired, because it was hard to get stuck in the mud with a horse and sled; for the first few years we didn't even have a horse. On occasion, we threw a few rocks in a small mud hole beside Jim Smith's peanut field. As time passed and automobile traffic increased, the small mud hole became the Big Mud Hole and a whole different animal. (It was located along the section of our road seen in the preceding photo.)

The mud hole ate rocks faster than we could haul them on the sourwood sled and just like fish worms in July, they went straight to China: never to be seen again. Rumor had it that a couple of cars may have disappeared, "right there in broad daylight: right before your very eyes, right on our road."

When at it's worst, I could no longer ride my bicycle all the way through without winding up stuck square-dab in the middle." Whether I wrecked, drowned, got covered with mud or all three, I knew Mama was waiting at home with a stern look on her face. She was the only person I knew who, without saying a single word, said it all.

The tire tracks were deep ruts on each side, with the middle scraped flat by dragging car bottoms. When a car's wheels dropped into the ruts, there was no way out except at the other end. Even with a good running start, it was almost impossible to drive all the way through without getting stuck in the middle of "the biggest mess you ever seen."

If a driver had been there before, he drove up to the mud hole, took a deep breath, got a good grip on his jug, his teeth and the steering wheel, revved the motor wide open and dived in. Metal-bending sounds could be heard a mile away, along with words unfit for tender ears. Muddy water sprayed far out on both sides of the road and when the car came to a stop, as most of them did, the driver had two choices: sit there and cuss or wade knee-deep mud to dry ground.

The rusted-out remains of an old car sat beside the mud-hole. Since I already knew everything about everything on Earth, it was just part of the scenery and I never asked what kind it was or how it got there. (People as smart as me didn't go around asking dumb questions.) Most likely, somebody got stuck; left the car there, walked away and never came back. Some people who got stuck got mad enough to do just that.

During the Big War, Beulah School held a scrap metal drive and I hauled parts of the old car to school on the bus. A small pile of scrap metal in the schoolyard soon became as big as a house and the teachers bragged so much about how good we'd done, I figured Beulah School won WW2 all by it's self. (Rumor had it that we sold the scrap metal to the Japanese, who made it into bombs and threw it back at us.)

Walking through the woods alone at night was, to say the least, frightening: especially with no moon, flashlight or lantern. I'd heard some crashing, thrashing noises that sounded like something as big as a horse was destroying the woods. It scared the daylights out of me and I desperately needed to be somewhere else: anywhere else. Whatever it was, I hoped and prayed it didn't know I was there, even though I was almost certain it did.

Running in the dark without a light was *not* the thing to do, because barbed wire fences and tree limbs were hard to see and they fought back when you tackled them. Climbing a tree wasn't a good idea either when it was too dark to find one. Worst of all, you couldn't tell if whatever was chasing you was gaining on you when it was too dark to see it.

I'd never thought about being scared in open places like the Big Mud Hole area, until going home alone one dark night. A strong wind was blowing from the mountain and it was hard to stay in the road, which I could hardly see. I was feeling my way along beside Jim Smith's peanut field, (with no light, as usual) trying not to think about scary things, but thinking of exactly that. When a small lightweight drawbar pole from the fence gate hit me in the face, the word "panic" does not begin to describe my feelings.

Cold chills as big as baseballs jumped off my back and headed for the hills and my hair headed for the stars. I grabbed the pole, held on tightly and tried to not think about what might be on the other end. It was too dark to run, so I just stood quietly and had another silent conversation with my Maker: one of many over the years.

When I finally remembered what Pa had said about that area, my heart slowed down to almost normal, "Windiest damn ridge I ever seen," I eased the small pole down to the ground and eased on toward home very quietly. I've never been quite sure what happened that night, but to this day, I still pray it was the wind.

On another night at a later time, I was again walking along in the same area after dark: not exactly scared, but very aware, wide-awake, saucer-eyed and by then: experienced. As always, I had no light and had just eased through the worst part of the Big Mud Hole and thought to myself, "Boy, I got it made." Almost immediately, a weird something about three feet long and a foot high came slithering along the ground toward me. It made no noise and neither did I, because my voice had had found other things to do in other places.

It was too dark to tell much about it, but whatever it was had no legs, it was moving and we were about to meet. Animals normally went out of their way to avoid people, but whatever it was, animal or otherwise, it was coming my way and it knew I was there.

With a blackberry briar thicket on the right roadside and Jim Smith's overgrown barbed wire fence on the left, there was nowhere to run except back through the Big Mud Hole. It was either drown in mud, get torn all to heck in a briar patch, die of fright, or stand my ground and fight no telling what. With nothing to throw but mud, I was in big trouble.

Just at the point of a heart attack, our dog whimpered as it crawled along on its belly: just as afraid of me as I was of it. I'd never been in better company as we walked on home in the dark. I later realized what a shame it was our own dog was that afraid of me. Never again did I walk easy in the Big Mud Hole area at night.

I planned to grow up, get rich, buy a Piper Cub airplane and use Jim Smith's peanut field for a landing field. (The field was too short for a landing field, but in my world, facts never stood in the way of a good daydream.) When Jim's wife Carrie died, he moved away and Pa bought his farm at auction. We then owned the peanut field and things were looking up.

Nobody on Stewart's Creek worried much about soil conservation; when a field completely wore out, everybody did as their fathers and grandfathers had done before them: they cleared off another new-ground. "Who's got time and money to mess with all that high-falutin' soil-savin' stuff? That's for them city-slicker farmers what ain't got nothing better to do no how."

One memorable year, Pa broke tradition and tackled soil improvement head-on when he bought a truckload of lime. He had it dumped near the Big Mud Hole and it didn't improve our land any at all, because none of it was ever moved. It became the next-best thing to a sandbox and local kids spent many happy hours building lime castles and digging holes in the big white mound. After a few years of playing, wind, rain and traffic, it gradually disappeared and in the meantime, we cleared off another new-ground.

(When the first Social Security check came in the mail, Pa retired from the heavy farming and leased his tobacco allotment to others. Except for tending the garden and growing tomatoes, he was a man of leisure and was never broke again.)

A driveway beside the lime pile led through a stand of locust trees that bloomed in odd years: some white and some purple. Honeybees worked on both kinds and didn't care what color they were. Locust honey was said to be almost as good as sourwood, but to me, it was all just plain good old honey.

The driveway continued beside Jim's "bob" wire fence to a one-room log cabin called the Hiatt House: named for the Alfred Hiatt family that once lived there. Roby and Sarah Smith built the house and a tobacco barn around 1920 and their oldest son Hurley was born there in 1922. Oscar and Lillie Marshall then bought the house and land and moved there from what they called their "Old House" on Stewart's Creek.

With the spring so far away, Oscar hired Pa, Bill Whitaker and others to dig a well. When they struck solid rock, they tried everything, including dynamite, but never found water. Oscar and Lillie then built their new two-story house (The New House) in a valley near his brother Little Sid. It was one of the nicest homes in our part of the country and Oscar said they could dip water from the spring with a long handled gourd and never leave the kitchen.

They then bought another home in Lambsburg and moved there. As the years passed, other families, including mine, lived in the New House for brief periods of time, but like the Hiatt House, it mostly sat empty.

My painting of the Hiatt House (1977)

I too was born in the Hiatt House, October 14, 1932: some ten years after Hurley Smith and according to Mama, there were better places to live. We had no well, electricity, screen doors, no under-pinning and no outhouse. We also had no horse, wagon, sled, cow, or money and at first, "no nothin'," as Mama said it.

Having very little money, renters either sharecropped the owner's fields, helped him make moonshine, or do other odd jobs. Some cabin owners charged no rent at all and thanks to Oscar Marshall, that was the going rate at the Hiatt House. Even without paying rent, neither we nor anyone else lived there very long.

The biggest problem was the spring being so far away. As my parents said it, "The spring was way down yonder in Walter Marshall's Woods and it wern't no fun a'tall a' totin' water from the other side a' nowhere." Jim and Farley Smith's springs were about the same distance away, which made water precious stuff. A fifty-gallon barrel under the house eave caught rainwater for washing clothes and bathing, but all other water was carried from the spring.

Lack of a bath wasn't the social disgrace it later became and some men took none at all. "A bath's the biggest water waster of all and you gotta' carry it a mile. Anybody wants a bath, let 'em stand out in the rain or go jump in the creek. I don't smell nothin' no-how." (When you met one of them in the dark at midnight, you knew who it was, sight unseen.)

Jim's "bob wire" fence offered the only protection from the fierce winter winds that roared down off Sugar Loaf Mountain. ("From straight outta' Bobbitt Holler' and you can it a' coming," according to Pa.) A very truthful person who once lived there said, "Livin' in the Hiatt House was worser than livin' in a barn, 'cause a barn's got hay to keep you warm. That wind, she blowed right in the cracks in one wall and right out the cracks in the other wall. I went in the back door one day and she blowed me right out the front door. A 'nother time she blowed the mud right outta' the cracks and blowed the dog plumb out from under the house. One 'a them bob' wires broke one winter night and we might near froze to death."

The same reliable source (who lived at the foot of the cross, by the way) told of another family who "got fancy" and chinked the cracks in their cabin walls with corn shucks instead of mud. "One cold winter night, a stray cow et' the shucks right out from between the logs and it was a week 'afore them people got thawed."

We lived in the Hiatt House for a year, then moved to the Fred Marshall house a half-mile away on the south side of Jim's Knob. Other families lived in the Hiatt House for brief periods: including Alfred Hiatt, but as time went by, it mostly sat empty, slowly went downhill and became a playhouse for kids and poker players. When the roof finally fell down inside, the Hiatt House was no more.

Just across the road stood a dilapidated log tobacco barn in a worn-out field of blackberry briars, broom straw, locust, and sassafras bushes. It had no door, the foundation had collapsed and the whole disaster leaned toward Jim's Knob. I never saw it used for anything, but a playhouse for kids. An Early Transparent apple tree grew nearby: with apples even earlier than Ed Smith's June Apples. Nobody had permission to get them, but when no one lived in the Hiatt House, whoever got there first got the apples and it was usually us.

Continuing along our road, a footpath turned right beside another barbed wire fence that led west to the Lambsburg Road. We used it as a "shortcut" to Walter Marshall's house and about half-way along it was a small hollow we ran down into and coasted up the other side: making loud motor noises. (The more noise you made, the faster you could run and it took lots of horsepower to lug a big load up the other side.)

Walter's three youngest kids: Avon, Russell and Gaynell, my brother Warren and I picked blackberries beside the path. We had a great time until some tiny red varmints called chiggers began eating me alive. They lived on berry vines and when I even got near a blackberry vine or a huckleberry bush, I got "all eat up." Certain places couldn't be scratched in polite company and when my hands got covered with berry juice, those were exactly the places that itched worst of all.

The same happened when working in tobacco: when my hands got covered with black tobacco gum, everything I had started itching and the more I couldn't scratch, the worse it itched. It was a great relief to back up against a tree or the barn and start rubbing when nobody was looking.

We had a neighbor who didn't want "them there wires run across my land," which caused a big delay in our getting electricity. When REA finally ran power lines along our road, new huckleberry bushes and blackberry vines grew in the right-of-way: with more chiggers. (Good scouts and hunters learned early on to keep an eye out for food at all times, even if it meant getting "eat plumb up" when they found it.)

Electricity brought an end to heating wash water and cooking with wood and we no longer used the kerosene lamp. The single bulb hanging from the ceiling gave enough light to read anywhere in the house, even at midnight. A new refrigerator brought an end to using the spring box and in 1955, a new well pump brought an end to winding well water. It took a while, but slowly and surely we began climbing out of the deep hole we started in.

My painting of the tobacco barn

The power lines continued to Grandpa's old place in the valley, which by then had been sold to Tom Senter. That brought an end to our using Grandpa's tobacco barns and with the help of neighbors and a barn raisin', we built our own barn on the hilltop beside our road.

It was made of logs, had a tin roof, (which would "last a lifetime if you died when you ought to) and a rusty fifty-gallon barrel under the drip-line to catch rainwater. The water came in handy when the flue fires got too hot and we made mud with it to daub the flue pipes. Mosquitoes laid eggs in the water that soon became "wiggle tails" that soon became new mosquitoes that soon ate me alive.

We had two tobacco sleds to haul the primed tobacco from the fields to the barn. The sides were made of burlap fertilizer bags with "S D" logo printed on them: the trademark of the Smith Douglas Company that manufactured the fertilizer. When we cured tobacco all night, we slept in the sleds to stay safe from snakes.

When Pa cured tobacco, he fired the barn so hot it was almost impossible to stay inside long enough to check the temperature and it felt good to get back outside and breathe again. We cut huge stacks of flue wood ahead of time, but when the curing began, they vanished into thin air.

One Saturday, a foxhunter blew his fox horn all night beside the barn and Pa said he thought about going up there and showing somebody "where to put that cow horn." The hunter came by next morning, apologized and said he was trying to keep his dogs out of our tobacco field and if he'd known tobacco was already that big, he would not have been foxhunting.

I stayed all night with Pa when he cured tobacco at Grandpa's barns, but when our new barn was built, I was older and wiser, Pa was older and dumber and I didn't stay with him much. When I began working in town, my farming days came to an end, then something strange happened: the farm kept right on going, even without my help.

I married, moved away and got older and dumber, as Pa got older and wiser. There actually came a time when we could walk through his fields, find the last tomato of the year, solve all the world's problems and laugh about the good old days. I never figured out how that happened.

A road led from the barn, through Oscar Marshall's Woods and continued beside Jim Smith's "bob-wire" fence. I once shot a hornet's nest hanging on the fence with Pa's shotgun. The hornets came boiling out mad as hornets and one flew straight back and stung me right between the eyes. Nobody had told me hornets could do that. Apparently, they'd never heard what a great hunter I was. Quick learner that I was, especially where pain was concerned, I never shot another hornet's nest or any other kind, for that matter.

Another road led south from the barn to our South Forty Woods, (a few acres.) My brother Warren's Boot Hill was somewhere in that area: where he "planted" all the people he'd "done away with" over the years, including most of our neighbors and he often threatened me. When a traveling salesman burned us in a rug deal, Pa told the next one that came by, "I got one of your kind planted up yonder in Boot Hill." He left so fast we never got a chance to invite him to supper.

The wintertime nightmare beside the tobacco field (2011)

Our road continued down a hill (seen above) that was no big deal in the early years, but as time passed and traffic increased; it became as bad or worse than the Big Mud Hole. Cars could go downhill o k, but going back up was almost impossible. To have any chance at all of climbing the hill, people backed their vehicles out to the feed barn to get a good running start. With a grim, determined look on their face and the bit in their teeth, they "floored-boarded it" and came roaring back by the house wide open.

Warren, the dog and I chased them around the curve to see if they made it up the hill. With three-foot high road banks and deep ditches on each side, there was no way to avoid the deep muddy ruts and no matter how fast they tackled the hill, most only made it about half way. What fun it was to see mud and smoke fly, as people sat there spinning and burning their tires off.

When *I* began driving, getting stuck was nowhere near as funny and I did it several times. Since I couldn't say bad words around my parents, I just sat there and pouted and thought some very bad thoughts. (When Pa died in February 1984, the hill was so muddy, no one could drive up it until we spread several loads of gravel on it.)

Our best tobacco field was beside the road, (seen on the right above) which I helped dig out of the woods in the late 1930s. Pa pulled stumps and roots out with the horse and blasted the biggest stumps out with dynamite, while we dug out small roots and rocks. It was hard dirty work for the whole family, but it was the only way we could get a new field at that time.

We lived in the field all spring, summer and fall: plowing, planting, hoeing, worming; suckering, priming, sweating and cussing tobacco. When windstorms blew the stalks over, we set them back up straight, and when all the tobacco was primed, it became my job to chop the stalks down with a tobacco knife.

That was the best time of the year in a tobacco field, because once that job was done, there'd be no more work there until next year. "Boy, you be careful. That 'baccer knife'll cut your legs off and you gonna' look funny walking on your hands."

About halfway down the hill, a path led left through the woods toward Farley Smith's house. I never knew why, but it came to a dead end in an ivy thicket. Every other path I'd ever seen led from somewhere to somewhere else, but that one ended in the middle of the woods.

Farley's son Rufus and I decided to get rich by selling roasted peanuts and hand-whittled baseball bats. We got two poles nailed together for a store building and opened for business on the dead-end path. The first bat was never finished and the peanuts were long gone before we sold any. When electricity came along in later years, the right-of-way ran through the middle of our former store site and continued to Little Sid Marshall's house across the valley.

Another path just below the Dead-end Path led downhill to Oscar Marshall's New House in the valley. In the late 1930s, I saw Sid Jarrell walking along it, wearing a black suit and carrying books under his arm. He was headed to a neighbor's house to give reading lessons. Some of our older neighbors had never learned to read and Sid, who was a schoolteacher, tried to teach those who wanted to learn.

While living in the New House, Mama said I "showed up missing" one day and when she called and I didn't answer, she panicked. She searched the whole area and finally found me going up-hill on the path, near where our new log house would later be built.

Our parents had told us we could catch a bird by putting salt on its tail and that what I was trying to do. Try as we might, we never got close enough to put any salt on any tails. Long before old age and senility set in, we decided birds always flew when you got close and salt had nothing to do with it. We named the path "The Bird Path."

The Woodshed (2007)

Our woodshed stood just beyond the Bird Path: on the right side of the road. When acorns fell from a chestnut oak, they made loud noises on the tin roof all day and night. When a puff of wind came, so many fell at the same time, it sounded like a war had begun. The acorns bounced downhill into the pasture, where new oaks came up the next spring.

Keeping enough wood for the cook stove and heater was one of our hardest, most demanding jobs. We sawed a tree down in the South Forty, dragged it to the woodpile with the horse, sawed it up, split it up and sometimes stored some in the shed, which was never full, because nobody was that ambitious.

My family sawed, cut and split firewood at the "woodpile" for some 48 years. The chopping block was a sawed-off piece of a big tree, where we split firewood and cut off chicken and mud turtle heads. The area became covered with sawdust and woodchips that decayed as time went by and became a good place to dig fish worms. In the warm days of spring, we dug up the whole area hunting worms. In the middle of summer, they went so deep in the ground you had to dig a well to find any.

Pine knots gathered from Jim's Knob in October 1991

When a 'possum pine died, it decayed for years until nothing was left but the limb, trunk and root parts that were heavy with pitch. We called them pine knots and used them as kindling to start fires when we had no kerosene oil. They were everywhere on the backside of Jim's Knob: the remains of pine trees killed by a "wild fire" in the 1930s.

After electricity came along, Mama cooked meals on an electric stove. That improved the wood situation tremendously, but Pa said corn bread was never again as good as it was cooked on the wood stove.

Our original house as it may have looked when built in 1936.

Just beyond the woodshed stood our house: also on the right side of the road. It came into being when Grandpa and Grandma gave us twenty acres of land. Thanks to the help of a dozen neighbors and a house raisin', we became the proud owners of a brand-new one-room log cabin, as Mama put it, "On a God forsaken ridge way out yonder in the middle of nowhere."

As the years passed, it became home for Pa, Mama, and eventually five boys and never again as a family, did we live anywhere else. Although not exactly wealthy, we were no longer at the very bottom of the social ladder. My three younger brothers were born there, where the five of us grew up: working, fighting, playing and running wild in the woods. Mama said she grew up there too: trying to raise us.

Pa, our son Mike and Mama on the front porch at the home place on Banjo Lane (1970)

Chapter 5

Home

The three windows in our new log cabin were salvaged from an old house on Ed Smith's farm. They were flawed and made everything outside look all bent out of shape. Warren and I slept in the attic and with only one small window for ventilation, it got a little toasty up under the tin roof in summer and stayed that way into the wee hours. In winter, it was like an iceberg and we dived into bed and shivered until we got warm. When more rooms were added, we dived into bed *downstairs* and shivered until we got warm.

We had no window or door screens in the early years and had more flying varmints inside than outside. A fly swatter and pull-down sticky flytraps kept them somewhat under control and when Pa traded for a used screen door, we could almost breathe inside on hot days. "Slam that door easy when you go out, boys, 'cause we ain't got no money to buy no more."

The final edition of home

The single room had a bed, kitchen table, cook stove, a small wood heater, a cardboard wardrobe and a boxed-in stairway. As Pa said it, "They ain't room in here to cuss a cat." He and Ed Smith then built the first addition in the late 1930s: a combination kitchen and bedroom on the back. It had no ceiling and was like sleeping at the North Pole. Mama called it a shed and said she had to "wrop' up good" on cold winter mornings to avoid freezing to death while cooking breakfast. She hung a blanket over the bed at night to keep out the cold wind, but it was still like sleeping outdoors.

As time passed, the family increased and a new kitchen, living room and mudroom were added, plus the "Little Room" on the front porch. With a wood heater, couch, chairs, bed, pedal sewing machine, wardrobe and a closet, the living room was over full. With a cook-stove, eatin' table, chairs and a bench, the kitchen was also full. When we added a refrigerator, we almost had stuff hanging out the window, especially when company came.

Absolutely nothing could be done without first checking Blum's Almanac and Kasco's Feed and Seed Store calendar. The latest copies of both hung on the wall and the almanac was worn dog-eared from checking moon signs. I once painted a picture of a sailing ship on a cracked 78-rpm record that hung on the wall for far more years then it deserved.

The house was never painted during the 48 years my family lived there, but Verlon Marshall under-pinned it with cinder blocks when he came home from the navy in the 1940s. When prosperity paid us another visit, we nailed screen wire over the windows to keep out some more of "them cussed varmints."

With mattock, shovel, wheelbarrow, sweat and manpower, we dug a basement under the new kitchen. Mama filled it with canned stuff, Irish potatoes and apples every summer and kept her potted flowers there in winter. At selling time, we hung sticks of cured tobacco in the basement to dampen, so it could be handled without crumbling.

With a thundering herd of elephants tromping on our linoleum rugs, they had a limited lifetime and needed replacing often. It took so much furniture moving, measuring, cutting, swearing and sweating, replacement time was a dreaded time. We once bought two nine by twelve rugs from a traveling salesman who assured us they would make one eighteen by twenty-four feet and cover the living room floor. After some more yardstick wars, discussions and combat, we could only make one eighteen by twelve or twenty-four by nine feet. (I'm not sure we ever figured it out.)

We finally figured out we'd "been took" and when the next salesman came by, Pa told him one of his buddies was buried in Boot Hill up yonder at the barn. The salesman cut off his sales pitch in mid-stream, headed for greener pastures and never again did we buy anything from a traveling salesman.

Rossie Golding ground our corn into cornmeal at his mill on Lambsburg Road. Either Grandpa hauled it on his wagon or we hauled it on horseback or "toted a turn" on foot: with the flour sack of shelled corn draped across our shoulders. (On the way back, the new meal was hot on bare shoulders.) We bought flour at Kasco's Feed and Seed Store in Mt. Airy and stored both it and the meal in a homemade meal "chist," (chest) on the kitchen porch.

We parked muddy shoes and dirty work clothes there and Mama dried the wash there on rainy days. A tin-door pie safe sat in the corner, but it never saw the first pie, because pies didn't hang around our house long enough to store. In fact, they never made it out of the kitchen. (The safe was our only mouse-proof storage place.) Strings of leather britches (air-dried green beans) hung from the rafters and tomatoes ripened on a narrow shelf. When we bought a new wringer washer, it too found a home on the porch.

I sat on the porch steps and practiced aiming my rifle at different targets. (Aiming was cheaper than shooting.) When a bird landed in a treetop, I took careful aim, pulled the trigger and it fell to the ground. Killing something we didn't eat gave me a bad feeling and I shot no more birds.

While aiming another day, a small plane flew by some distance away. Bingo! Another Japanese Zero was about to go "you-know-where in a ball of fire." "Captain Easter" was on the job and aimed above and in front of the plane to allow for windage, speed, height and distance, as us experts were trained to do. I gently pulled the trigger, as us experts were trained to do and when the rifle fired, the airplane didn't go down in flames, but I did.

I'd forgotten it was ready to shoot and when it fired, it scared me out of my wits. I could already see smoke, fire, explosions, crashes and other major disasters happening right there before my very eyes. I could also see the newspaper headlines, "Famous scout and hunter dies of heart failure after pot-shot at airplane." For sure, Pa and me would soon be doing another of his hickory-switch dances. I breathed a huge sigh of relief as the plane continued on its merry way and knew for a fact: I'd just bagged my last airplane.

When Pa and Mama built our new house, they set a dozen white pines on the west side to grow into a windbreak. (The prevailing winds came from that direction.) As time passed, the pines grew tall but the wind still "blowed us away." It almost never stopped in winter and when it did, we could still hear it roaring in the mountain.

The grindstone

Our first piece of equipment stood across the road from the windbreak white pines: a hand-powered water-cooled (also by hand) grindstone. The cement wheel and handle were mounted on a wooden frame fastened to a shade tree. Pa sharpened our axes, hoes and knives, while Warren and I turned the handle and kept the wheel wet with water.

We chopped wood continually and Pa's "good" axe needed sharpening often. When he asked, "Who's been chopping my axe in the ground?" Warren and I said," Not me. Not me." As my three younger brothers grew up, they said: "Not me. Not Me. Not Me."

We had just sharpened the axe and while leaning on the handle, I stepped back against the newly sharpened blade and cut my bare foot severely. With the closest doctor "plumb over the mountain," Doctor Mama went to work, stopped the bleeding and wrapped my foot with so much stuff I could hardly walk. Thanks to her and the magic qualities of Iodine, it healed.

Mercurochrome was better than Iodine, because it didn't burn and the bigger the area covered by the red cure-all, the more important it looked. Even a minor wound was impressive when covered with a big red smear. "Hey, everybody: look how bad I got hurt."

I read that the North Star stayed at the same place in the sky and sure enough, there it was every night: right over the big white pine, right across the road. Except for the sun, the moon and the planets, everything else in the sky rotated completely around it once in a year's time. That made any particular star or constellation visible only at certain times of the year and by knowing some of the major stuff, I could tell if it was winter or summer by just looking up in the sky.

Pa, who was no scientist like me, said he could tell that a whole lot easier by looking at the calendar and by how cold or hot it was. (Some people didn't appreciate the technical things us experts had to know. It would take a while, but I planned to learn every star in the sky and be the best weather forecaster anybody ever heard tell of.)

When I looked up one winter night, my normal sky was no longer there, as red streaks of light covered the Heavens: all the way from overhead to Sugar Loaf Mountain. A local preacher had told us the end of time was coming and if we didn't go to church, we'd see fire and brimstone. All of a sudden, there it was, right up there over the trees. I broke out in a cold sweat and thought about running, or at least doing something: anything. With no idea what to do or which way to run, I just stood there scared to death until I remembered reading about the Northern Lights.

Pa knew what it was all along, "Them Japs is a' comin' boys, you better light out fer' the hills. They done broke through the line and they'll be here by mornin' a' droppin' them bums' everywhere." (Concerning world affairs, Pa was always right up on the cutting edge.)

I saw a faint comet one night: high over the mountain, apparently headed toward Jim's Knob. I'd read that comets traveled thousands of miles an hour but anybody could see it was standing still. I watched for several nights and it just sat there in the same place.

I'd heard a Gospel song with the words, "A band of Angels coming after me; coming for to carry me home." While playing in the yard one summer day, the Angels began singing that very song: "right up there in the sky: right over our house." I looked all over everywhere, couldn't see a thing and ran inside scared half to death. It was a fact of life staring me straight in the face; the Angels were "coming for to carry me home." The same preacher who'd told us the end of time was coming, also told us we'd go to Hell in a hand-basket and burn in the fiery furnace. When the Angels began singing, I could already smell the smoke.

I was basically a good person, but it looked like my rabbit's foot had done run out of luck and the last thing I needed was a trip into the sky without an airplane. Pa and Mama and our little corner of the world suited me just fine just like it was. They probably didn't even have fishing holes up there. Everybody deserved another chance and if the Angels would just give me one more, I'd do a whole lot better: maybe even go to church next Sunday.

Mama finally got me calmed down and told me it wasn't the Angels singing; just an auctioneer named Golly "Stanley" (Stantliff) riding the back roads in his car playing gospel music on a loudspeaker. Who ever heard of such a thing? It was a great relief to know I didn't have to go yet, but ever after, I kept a close eye on Golly anytime he was near me.

Our house had no chimney when first built: just a stovepipe stuck out through the wall. C L York later built one made of bricks on the east end and when the new living room was added, the chimney was in the middle of the house. It never needed cleaning, because Pa fired the heater so hot, creosote was afraid to form. Just like the radio and later the t v, the heater had only one speed: "wide open." The heat and noise were enough to drive the whole family mad, especially Mama, who was home all the time.

Pa in his favorite chair by the wood heater

Our first wood heater was made of tin and Pa fired it "as hot as she'll run" as he did its cast-iron replacement. (Seen above.) An untold number of trees went up the chimney in the 48 years my family lived there but we never ran out. One local family actually burned all their trees for heat and cooking, but thanks to caring neighbors, they had firewood.

Pa always kept the living room warm in winter, but as he got older, it was like living in an oven. He sat as close to the heater as possible, kept his cigar smoking like a freight train and the heater jumping a foot off the floor. He stayed warm and content, while everybody else died from cigar smoke and the heat. It was a wonder he didn't burn the house down.

Before we bought a radio, we borrowed a wind-up tabletop record player from my aunt. It came with a hand-full of needles that never wore out, but Warren and I replaced them continually. (How could anybody know how good we were at technical things, unless they saw us in action?) We played the same songs over and over until it was no longer fun, then parked the player in the attic: which Pa and Mama thought was the best idea we'd ever had.

The attic was our junk room, where we threw everything we had no other place for. We had no lamp there, but a small window on the west end gave enough light to read by and I spent many happy hours beside it: completely lost in books. Even after leaving home, I dreamed of reading by the window on rainy days.

Some three years before electricity came along, we made a huge jump into the modern world; Pa bought a battery-powered radio from Robert Smith, who had just got home from the Big War. We then had magic coming to our house just like Jim Smith and we didn't need an "earl" wire tied to an apple tree outside, because ours was "built-in."

The music was so much better than the scratched, worn-out records we'd played and never again were we without a radio, until the batteries died. Then, everything got quiet around the old homestead, until Pa and Mama held another discussion of each other's lousy idiotic ancestors. Then, things got very loud. When new batteries finally came in the mail, everything soon got back to normal.

Hearing my heroes in action was almost as good as reading about them in a book. The highlight of the day was getting the chores done so we could listen to our favorite programs: Lum and Abner, Amos and Andy and the Lone Ranger. To conserve the batteries, we only played the radio at low volume, the thinking being, it took more "juice" to play it louder. (That was actually true.)

Pa liked country music, weather reports, and a news program called the Esso Reporter. Two of his favorite stations were WJJD Chicago and WWVA Wheeling, West Virginia. On cold winter mornings, he gave us his weather report, "It's cold as Hell out there in Chicago."

As he grew older, his hearing went downhill and the radio volume went up: often so loud it was impossible to carry on a conversation. I asked him one day (loudly) to turn it up a little; he didn't turn it down. (He probably didn't hear me.)

My ticket to Nashville

After hearing some great songs on the radio, I decided to become a Big Star on the Grand 'Ole Opry'. All them people had to do was play the guitar and sing and I was already a great singer. When I found a magazine ad that promised to teach guitar playing in a "dozen easy lessons or double your money back," I jumped on it with both feet. I'd hire somebody to hoe corn in the hot summer fields, while I played the guitar, lived in Nashville and brought fame and fortune to Stewart's Creek. I traded for a used guitar (seen above) and ordered the book, knowing good times were just around the corner. The world had never seen a guitar player like I'd be.

The book finally came, I learned a few chords and did what I thought was a great job of "playing a tune." I played and played and sang (loudly) for a very long time and finished driving my parents mad. I kept an eye on the sky, the mailbox, and everything I could think of, but for some reason, Nashville never called. (As a keeper of the faith to this day, my guitar stands ready in my closet; you can never tell when the call might come.)

When REA finally pulled power line across the hills, two huge changes came into our lives: our kerosene lamp and battery powered radio days came to a screeching end. It was unbelievable that two wires tied to a power pole out in the pasture could make such a change in how we lived. The single light bulb hanging from the ceiling was even brighter than Walter Marshall's carbide lights and we didn't have a smelly carbide storage tank in the back yard. (Fact of the matter, we had very little of anything in the back yard.) The light bulb didn't smoke, smell, or need cleaning. It burned no kerosene oil and best of all, it burned no wood and instead of one best place to read, I could read anywhere in the house at any time: even at midnight.

We bought a new electric radio that had no batteries to run down and our listening hours increased dramatically. We hurried to get the chores done and get back to our favorite programs. Sadly, there was never enough time to listen to everything we wanted to hear.

Radio station WPAQ Mount Airy came on the air on Groundhog Day, February 2, 1948: with news and weather reports about *our* part of the country. Uncle Joe Johnson and Pretty Blue-eyed Odessa played guitars and sang, Uncle Henry played records and we listened every chance we got.

We'd come a long way since the 1930s, when the whole neighborhood gathered at Jim Smith's house on Saturday nights to listen to the Grand Ole' Opry on his battery powered radio. We now had electricity and a power bill of $1.50 each month. It was our first experience with a monthly bill and was sometimes hard to pay. (When we bought an electric stove and a refrigerator, we paid more.)

Except for Big Mike who died in 1964, my brothers and I grew up and went our separate ways. Neither of us became farmers, which broke some long-standing traditions in our part of the Easter Clan. Helen and I lived in Mount Airy, but my other three brothers, except for short periods of time, lived in the area where we grew up.

They kept an eye on the old folks and when a major calamity happened: such as running low on firewood, they were the first to know. I helped when possible, but never as much as they did because they lived close by. Thanks to them, Pa never ran out of firewood, which was one of his greatest fears in his later years.

Pa splitting kindling (From a 1960s home movie)

The Home Place in the 1970s

The Home Place

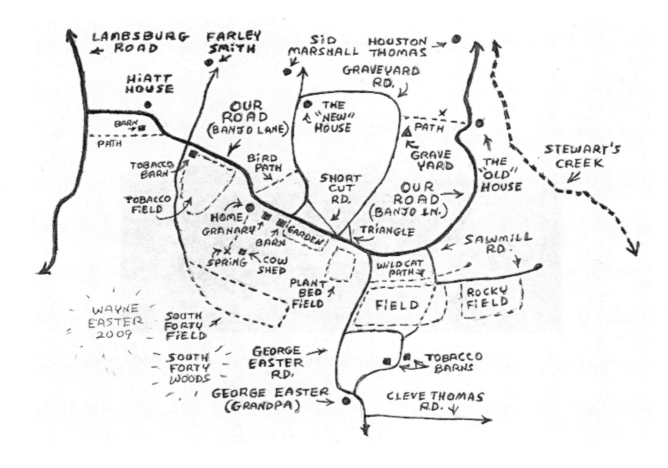

Chapter 6

The Home Place

Home (1955)

We were never without a job as we cleared new grounds, ploughed the land, repaired fences and cut firewood eight days a week. When Pa decided which way a tree would fall, he chopped a notch on that side and told me, "Be ready to run if it don't fall right" (They always fell where he aimed them.) We chopped off the limbs, dragged the trees home with the horse and sawed them into stove wood.

We kept our fences mended and our animals stayed home, but some of our careless neighbors let a "whole passel of hellions" as Pa called them, came calling to "eat us plumb outta' house and home." When a stray animal came by, he broke out Old Betsy and "put some more lead in some more hides." (If he'd actually shot everything that came by, we would've had no friendly neighbors and even so, some of them looked at us a little funny anyway: especially those who didn't mend their fences.)

A dozen locust trees grew in the pasture, with thorns that went deep into bare feet and what with bee stings, stone bruises and stumped toes, tender bare feet lived a hard life in early spring. By mid-summer, that was no longer a problem; we could almost stomp rocks.

Our first garden was fenced, but when the wire rusted away, we had no money for new wire and started a new unfenced garden on the hill beside the barn. That's when the fun began, as every stray animal from "you-know-where and half a' Georgia" moved in.

We carried water from the spring, two buckets at a time, which took half as many trips and we could almost walk level. It was a man-killing job we did for many years and as the spring path wore deeper, the buckets dragged on the ground: just like my tongue when carrying water up the hill.

We cooled milk, butter, watermelons and other foods in a spring box that straddled the spring branch. When heavy rains came, a river of muddy water came pouring downhill and flooded the box: causing the food containers to float around inside. We learned early on to seal everything up tight, because nobody liked muddy water for supper.

To avoid carrying water up the hill, Mama washed clothes at the spring when weather permitted. She placed the washtub on three rocks, built a fire under it, boiled and washed the clothes and hung them on the garden fence to dry. For all other purposes, we carried water up to the house, including a once-a-week bath in the washtub. Dirty or not, we got a good scrubbing behind the ears and everywhere else.

Mama also canned beans and scalded chickens and 'possums in the washtub and when not in use, it hung on a nail on the outside wall. It made a great noise when hit with a stick, but she told us, "If you all don't quit beatin' on my poor old washtub, I ain't gonna' have no poor old washtub."

As time passed, the distance to the spring increased tenfold and we bugged Pa about a well, "Other people got wells, so why ain't we got one?" His reply, "It takes money to drink likker' and ride the train, boys and we ain't got none." (He was usually right about the money and he also didn't have to carry water up the steep hill.)

Around 1940, Bud Crotts hand-dug our well just outside the kitchen door. To avoid walking back and forth to Lambsburg each day, he slept in our barn at night. Well-digging was man-killing work: even harder than carrying water from the spring, but with determination, mattock and shovel, he headed for China. We wound him in and out of the hole with a windlass and rope, wound out the dirt and used it to level the back yard.

After some hard sweaty days, Bud struck water and brought an end to carrying water from the spring: one of the best things that ever happened on our hill. Spring water was said to be better than well water, but right off the bat, we had "the best well water God ever made." For the first few days, winding water was the greatest thing going, but in a few more days, the new wore off and nobody wanted to wind water.

With the coming of electricity, we bought a new refrigerator and quit using the spring box. We continued winding water from the well until the spring of 1955. I'd just got home from the army and liked sleeping late on my days off. When Mama rousted me out of bed one Saturday to wind up wash water, I brought a well pump from Shelton Plumbing in Mt Airy. After some backbreaking work and family wars, we finally had running water in the house. Nobody complained about the end of winding water from the well, especially me. (The Bud Crotts well failed in 1982 and Newman Brothers Well Company bored a new one with a well-drilling machine.)

When blackberries ripened in mid-summer, we headed for the great outdoors with our Beulah Buckets. (Gallon-sized tin vegetable cans that came from the Beulah School lunchroom.) They were free and made good flowerpots, berry buckets, garden buckets and pretty good drums for budding musicians.

Mama made blackberry pies and blackberry jelly and we sold some at Rossie Golding's store. (I usually ate more berries than I picked.) What we really did at the store was trade berries for stuff we needed and I usually needed some candy. Other local storeowners who bought berries were: Bert Ward in Lambsburg, Sid Jarrell at Crooked Oak Crossroads and Cosby Golding in Round Peak.

On occasion, a rock defied the law of gravity and jumped into somebody's berry bucket. Storeowners frowned on trading candy for rocks and watched for extra heavy buckets. When they found one, they removed the rock and re-weighed the berries. The bucket owner was never at fault, "I don't know how that rock got in there." No rocks were ever found in *our* berry buckets, because we'd already been threatened with bodily harm for much lesser crimes. Compared to some of the neighborhood kids, Warren and I lived at the foot of the cross.

Mama made jelly and jam from Concord grapes and Pa made wine. Grandpa stored his wine in kegs in the smokehouse, but Pa's didn't hang around long enough to store anywhere. Just like his peach brandy, moonshine and home-brew, his evaporated into thin air.

Under threat of bodily harm, we were forced to take Black Draught: the worst tasting stuff God ever made. Second worst was Pa's homebrew, which tasted worse than something that had died last year. Best I could tell, his taster was all out of whack, because he smacked his lips and said, "That's the best stuff I ever seen." Just like his moonshine; he could "drink'er straight down" without frowning.

Our chickens ran free in the daytime, scratched up everything in sight and laid eggs everywhere except where they were supposed to: in a row of nests on the back of the granary. They roosted in the chicken house at night, to stay safe from weasels and other varmints.

Pa was always at war with the chicken hawks that ate our widdies and the suck-egg dogs that ate our eggs. When either of them showed up, he fired up "Old Betsy" and almost never missed. As he said it, "You can't run a farm without a shotgun,"

My favorite food, bar none, was fried chicken and I never had enough except on Foot-washing Day at Crooked Oak Church. When we needed one to eat, we first had to catch it and that took the whole family and the dog. Chickens were already the fastest things on earth but when we tried to "run one down," it broke the sound barrier. It squawked, flapped and headed for far places as fast as it could go. With visions of fried chicken in the air, we never failed, but we got a little tired sometimes.

Pa then chopped the chicken's head off with the axe or Mama wrung its neck by whirling it around and around. She then dipped it in a washtub of boiling water to loosen the feathers, we "plucked" them off, she cleaned it out, cleaned it up, cut it up and finally, at long last, she fried it up, then we ate it up. I didn't care much for the plucking, the cleaning out or the cutting up, but when it came to the frying up and the eating up, I had no problem with any of that.

Chicken was best when fried, but Mama's chicken dumplings too, were food for the Gods. Everybody wanted a drumstick, but with a chicken only having two, it was hard to divide them among several people. Somehow, someway, it worked and one chicken fed the whole family. When company came, the Gods smiled big time and Mama fried two at the same time.

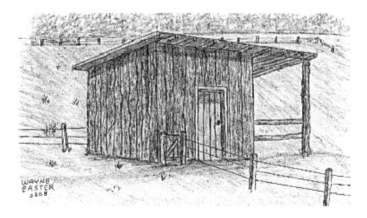

The "slab-sided" cowshed

The cowshed was made of slabs, had a tin roof and although not exactly airtight, it was better than no shelter at all. It was "way down yonder" in the holler' beside the first garden and unlike Grandpa and Jim Smith's cowsheds, it was taller than the cow and she could get inside without crawling.

Old Bossie wore no bell and was sometimes hard to find at milking time. While Mama was milking one day, she told me, "Don't let the calf get out of the shed." When it shook its head and headed my way, I headed for the hills. She said, "I told you to not let that calf out." I told her, "You'd run too, if a calf was a' headin' at you." (My brother Warren never let me forget how his big brave brother ran from a little calf.) We cooled the milk in the spring box until mealtimes; then up the hill it went. If any was left over, back down the hill it went and next day, we did it all over again.

The Necessary House (1971)

We had no necessary house for many years, because necessary houses were unnecessary on our hill: just another one of "them hi-falutin' things" for rich people. Mama and my brother Curtis finally built one made of sawmill slabs down on the hillside. In later years, he and my brother El installed a bathroom in the back bedroom, which brought an end to braving the great outdoors at midnight in mid-winter. (When the above photo was made, the outhouse had gone unused for many years.)

The "Grain-ry"

The "grain-ry," (granary) stood just beyond the house and like all of our buildings, it was on the right side of the road. It had a wood-shingle roof and weatherboard siding that was never painted and when the shingles wore out, Pa replaced them with tin. He stored his plows, 'baccer setter, crosscut saw, used lumber and some outdated license plates under the side-shelter.

He kept his hammer, handsaw, auger; plow wrenches, a ball of twine, Grandpa's corn sheller and a pair of pig wringers inside. (The wringers were used to put rings in pig's noses to keep them from rooting their way out of the pen.) He also kept his "good axe" inside when not being used and it was strictly off limits to all boys, always. Warren and I had our own axe to chop rocks, sticks and anything else that needed a good whacking. We left it where we used it last and could never remember where that was.

At hog-killing time, we "salted the meat down" in a meat box that sat in a corner. I once caught a cat inside the box eating on the fatback. I grabbed it by the tail, threw it against the wall and it never ate again. (Pa had taught his sons well; anything that messed with our winter's meat supply was in big-time trouble.")

Pa stored dynamite in a five-gallon lard-can in the granary loft and only had to tell us once, "That stuff'll blow you to Kingdom Come." (That was one warning we heard.) He used the dynamite to blow stubborn stumps out of the ground and "fished" with it. We never got "blowed away" and were never got overloaded with dynamited fish.

The granary door was made of rough planks and held shut with a metal hasp and a wooden peg. It was never locked, until Pa began hiding his jug inside. He then used an ancient rusty lock that probably came over on the boat with Grandpa's ancestors. To get it locked and unlocked took stronger language than "Open Sesame," but Pa had the words. He kept the key hidden exactly where the dumbest of crooks would look first: behind a double-shovel plow-point that hung on the outside wall: within inches of the lock and hasp.

We had apple trees, but never pruned or sprayed them and we had very few apples. As the old folks said it, "We used to have good crops of all that stuff without all that prunin' and 'a sprayin' and 'a messin'. All that changed when we started using all that high-price fertilize.' Way back yonder, we just stuck stuff in the ground and got outta' the way."

(After Russia launched Sputnik in 1957, crop failures and other disasters were blamed on "all that stuff they're shootin' up yonder in the sky." Pa never believed "all that space stuff," According to him, "They made them pictures out yonder in the Arizony Desert." In early spring, we dug fish worms under the apple trees, but by July, they were so deep in the ground, the Chinese were digging our worms.

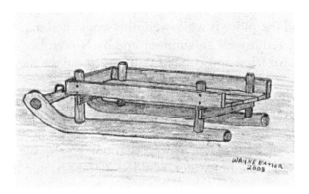

Sourwood sled

We had no transportation early on, unless we borrowed Grandpa's horse, wagon and sled. When Pa finally bought a horse, we searched the woods for two sourwood trees with sharp bends, found two the right size, cut them down, dragged them home with the horse and built our own sourwood sled.

We bored auger holes in the bent ends of each runner for a tongue, bored two more in each runner for up-right standards and nailed braces crossways between the standards. We then nailed planks on it lengthwise to help hold everything together. We hammered, measured, and sweated for hours, as Pa discussed the situation with words not found in the dictionary. We finally got it all together and were ready to "haul the mail" as he said it. Nobody ever had a finer sled and we no longer had to borrow Grandpa's.

The sled worked great until the horse was pulling it along the road one day, as Pa walked along behind. When he looked up at the sky to check the weather, the horse stopped, but Pa didn't. He fell forward on the sled and skinned both legs below his knees. An hour later, the air was still fogged up with high-powered words. As always, Pa won the war.

Warren and I laughed about the sled deal for a week, but when it happened to me, it was nowhere near as funny. I couldn't even bad-mouth the horse, not out loud anyway, because Easter kids were forbidden to even think bad words, let alone say them. (On the chance that Pa and Mama could read minds, I was even careful what I thought.)

Plowing was man-killing work and sometimes dangerous. If the plow hit a stump, root, or rock, it could stop instantly and cause a hard plow-handle blow to the ribs. Farmer Brown then became Astronomer Brown, as planets, stars and other heavenly bodies circled around right before his very eyes, right there in broad daylight.

Pa did it his own way and plowed with the plow lines looped around his neck and if the singletree broke or came loose, the plow always stopped but sometimes the horse didn't. That caused him to be dragged by the neck halfway over the plow handles. That created more problems that got worked out with the plow lines and a language only he and the horse understood.

Warren and I were never short on world-changing projects, but most were never finished because an even greater idea soon came along. Inspiration lit up the whole sky one day and we decided to build ourselves a wooden wheeled wagon. The world had never seen one such as ours and we might even sell some.

We sawed wheels from a black-gum tree, bored holes in them with the auger, made axles, a tongue and a bed. When fastened together, the whole thing didn't weigh quite a ton, but it came close. We hitched the calf to it, but neither calf nor wagon moved. It would almost roll downhill, but like so many other of our great inventions, it never got off the ground.

Pa bought a new pig each spring that stayed in a pen beside the granary. On hot summer days, it wallowed in a mud hole and the more it wallowed, the worse it stank. Nobody dilly-dallied around our hog pen, ever. We fed it well all summer and by November, it had grown into a fat hog. That meant more lard, which we fried and cooked with every day of the year. (Nobody wanted a skinny hog at killing time.)

Hog killing time came with the November frosts and one cold morning, we set up the scalding vat across the road from the granary, filled it with water and built a fire under it. When the water got hot, Pa shot the hog with a .22 rifle: one shot in the forehead "right between the eyes" and cut its throat with a butcher knife to "bleed it out." With a neighbor's help, we loaded it on the sled, hauled it to the scalding vat, rolled it into the hot water, scalded it and scraped the hair off with butcher knives.

Pa inserted a sharpened stick in the tendons of both back legs and using a block and tackle, hung the hog head down from a tree limb. He disemboweled it, washed it out, lowered it to some planks and made hams, shoulders and side meat with the ax and butcher knife right there on the spot. We "salted down" everything in the meat box and gave the neighbor a "mess of fresh meat." (When *he* killed *his* hog, he returned the favor.)

We made sausage just like Grandpa and Grandma: with a hand cranked meat grinder clamped to the kitchen table. We ground it into a dishpan, seasoned it with salt, sage, red hot pepper, formed it into round balls, fried and canned it for winter. Of all the stuff Mama canned, good old sausage was the best of all.

After all the fat was cooked out of the small pieces of meat, they became the cracklins' we cooked in corn bread: one of Pa's favorite foods. He also liked hog brains fried with scrambled eggs and sliced cured ("streak-id") raw fatback. He also liked 'possums, mud turtles and come to think of it, I don't remember much he didn't like in the eating department.

On hog-killing day, our whole hill smelled of grease and raw meat and even thinking about eating pork turned me wrong-side-outards. Next morning, Mama cured my problem with a breakfast of fried tenderloin, buckwheat pancakes, fried eggs and white-sop gravy.

The feed barn (1980s)

The feed barn was just beyond the hog pen: built in the mid-1940s with logs from Jim and Carrie Smith's old house on Lambsburg Road. We stored tobacco, fodder and tops inside and kept the horse in a stall around back. When Aunt Maude's husband Allen Seal died, she gave Pa their tractor and he parked under a shelter at back.

Our second garden was just beyond the barn and even being unfenced, it did well, even after I moved away. I too had a garden, but it never matched theirs. Pa said his onions were as big as a bucket and when I asked how he did it, he said. "Git you a' almanac, boy, and go by them signs."

We waded barefoot in a mud hole beside the garden and tried to see how far we could stomp water. "If you all don't stay outta' them mud holes, you gonna' catch warts, and the plague and no telling' what else playin' with them tadpoles." (With so many rules and regulations, it's a wonder we had any fun at all.) With very little automobile traffic in that area, the small mud hole never became a problem like the Big Mud Hole.

Every spring, we cleared off a new tobacco plant bed in land that had never been tended before. Last year's plant bed place was then added to what we called the Plant Bed Field. We were hoeing corn there one day, while Warren played under a shade tree. Pa told him, "Bring that hoe down here, boy." Warren didn't quite understand what Pa said and bounced down the hill making motor noises and saying, "Roll down, babe, roll down," without the hoe.

Pa turned him around with some kind words and a dose of hickory tea, "Git' your roll down blankety blank blank' back up yonder and bring that hoe down here, boy; you must be deaf as a post." Warren blazed a brand new trail back up the hill and performed the fastest hoe retrieval in history. I never let him forget that little incident.

After the frosts began, we set rabbit gums in the fields and woods, hoping to catch breakfast. According to Guy Haunn, it was a short-term deal, "You might as well bring in your gums after Christmas, 'cause them rabbits won't go in 'em after that."

We made gums from two-foot sections of a hollow log, fitted with a door, a back cover and a trigger. Some people made gums from lumber, which looked more "store-boughten," but we caught just as many rabbits as they did.

We checked them every day and sometimes caught a rabbit or a 'possum, but praise the Lord, no polecats like some people did. The door was closed on my gum one morning and when I looked inside, my first rabbit looked back at me. I shook it out into a fertilizer sack; it ran through a hole and headed for the hills. Since rabbits could run so fast, I didn't even try to catch it.

I told Pa, "If the sack hadn't had a hole in it, I'd a' caught a rabbit," He told me, "If the dog hadn't stopped to do you know what, it would'a caught a rabbit too." That didn't help my feelings any at all, but I checked all of our fertilizer sacks for holes.

Tracking rabbits in the snow was a great idea that didn't work very well, at least for me. I followed tracks all around brush piles and hollow logs and except for dogs, I never saw the first animal. Maybe they knew I was on their trail and walked backwards or something trying to confuse me. Whatever it was, it worked, because the Great Hunter never tracked anything down and everything was long-gone when I got there. That was no great problem; when it snowed again, I'd be back again and try again.

Our road continued beyond the garden to what we called the Triangle, where three roads came together. The Graveyard Road forked left to Oscar Marshall's New House in the valley and another short-cut road led to the same house. I once dug a pit on the short-cut road and covered it with sticks and leaves: trying to trap some (any) kind of animal. The pit was at least a foot deep and any self-respecting small puppy could've jumped out of it. Needless to say, I never caught anything and thank my lucky stars I didn't catch Pa.

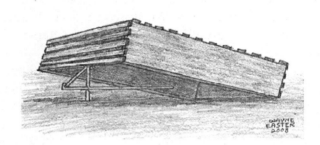

Bobwhite trap: with a figure-four trigger

Continuing beyond the Triangle, Grandpa's Road (The George Easter Road) forked right off our road, leading by his best up-land field. He grew corn and watermelons there every year and one particular year, he caught a neighbor stealing his watermelons.

When a covey of bobwhites flew out of the field one day, I had another brainstorm. I built a bobwhite trap from scrap lumber, made a "figure four trigger," put some corn under it for bait and placed it in the field. I just knew bobwhites would come flocking in by the dozens and I could almost taste fried bobwhites at breakfast.

One day the trap was down, several bobwhites were caught inside and all were alive except for one the trap had fallen on. I gathered all I could hold in my arms and some got away. More got away as I went home and I only made it back with two: including the dead one. When Mama asked why I hadn't killed them before starting home, it took all of the air out of my sails, because nobody had told me I had to kill them. My bobwhite-trapping days ended that very day and I even wished the dead one had flown away.

Beyond the George Easter Road, the Sawmill Road branched right off our road. My brother Curtis was riding his bicycle there one day and heard a wild cat screaming down a nearby path. He jumped off the bicycle and ran home scared out of his wits. Pa soon came home laughing about how he'd scared Curtis. (We named the path "The Wild Cat Path.")

Ivy (mountain laurel) was a small green shrub a few feet high that grew everywhere in the woods and no landowner cared who broke his ivy. In November and December, we just headed for the woods with fertilizer sacks to break ivy and earn some extra money. We broke a ton of it along the Wild Cat Path and strung it into the 50-foot lengths we sold to the T N Woodruff Company at Low Gap. The extra money was sometimes our only money and the only way Santa could come at Christmas.

The Sawmill Road continued south to the other end of Grandpa's field, (the same field where I set the bobwhite trap) turned left and led to his rocky field on the ridge above Stewart's Creek. The field was full of rocks, hard to plow and nothing grew well there. Warren and I had a great time rolling the rocks downhill into the Cleve Thomas Road, but we never cleared the field.

Our road continued beyond the Sawmill Road, downhill by Oscar Marshall's Old House on Stewart's Creek and up the valley to the Houston Thomas house. (When the county named every road, driveway and cow path known to mankind, our road became "Banjer' (Banjo) Lane.")

We'd heard about the Great Depression, but it brought no great changes in how we lived. As did our neighbors, we plowed the land, sowed the seeds and kept makin' likker'. Pa and Mama worked as best they knew how, trying to keep us clothed and fed. Mama made some of our clothes from flour sacks and tried to keep us looking halfway decent.

Keeping all the knee and seat of the pants holes patched was a full time job and she threatened to make us go to school "nekkid" if we didn't take better care of our clothes. (Who had time to worry about such stuff, when the whole world was waiting to be explored? When not in school or hoeing corn, we were running wild in the woods.)

For many years, our only transportation was by foot, horseback and the sourwood sled, but we didn't feel deprived. We knew all about walking and that was how we got where we went. Stewart's Creek was only a half-mile away and it took almost no time to dig some worms, get there and start fishing.

Having no money was no big problem, because most of our neighbors were just like us. Some may have been even poorer, because they had no horse or sourwood sled. Us plain ordinary folks didn't need "none a' them modern things" like an automobile, electricity or an outhouse. Outhouses were few in our world and we considered people who had them to be "a little uppity."

Few people in our world had an automobile and neither did we until 1948, when Pa bought a 1931 A Model coupe from Howard Hawks. For the first time ever, when we needed to go to the store, we didn't walk or ride the horse: we drove the car. Even bumming a ride to town became a thing of the past.

Pa was never an ace at driving, but managed to get where he wanted to go, even to Scrap Town to buy a case of moonshine. He later bought an A Model sedan and even later bought a pickup. He could then haul his own tobacco to the markets in Mount Airy, which he couldn't do with the A Models.

He often "had a little snort" while driving and sometimes had more than a little. He said his vehicle was trained to bring him on home when he needed to take a little nap. That may have been true, because he always got home safely, mostly because everybody stayed out of his way.

My brother Warren fixed up an old jalopy he called his "motorized sourwood sled." It had no muffler and you could hear it coming a mile away. He became the terror of the back roads and his favorite racetrack was Lambsburg Road.

One of his greatest joys was seeing how far into the woods he could throw gravel in Frank Coalson's Curve. The way he told it, "You see me coming, you better get out of the way, because I move more gravel than the N. C. Dept. of Transportation." (After one ride with him, I had absolutely no doubt about it.)

While home on leave, an army pal and I took a spin with him and while going uphill from Grandpa's old place, the jalopy quit running and began rolling back down the hill. Warren backed it out into a field and just as he got it stopped, my buddy jumped out. I was never allowed to forget "that big brave army guy" I brought home with me.

Warren, Pa and a load of tobacco on the jalopy

After Warren married and moved away, he was driving home one night, when a white ghost ran across the road at Zion Hill Cemetery. He hurried home, got his shotgun and drove back by the cemetery. When the ghost ran across the road again, he fired the shotgun into the air as it ran behind Crooked Oak Church. He stopped by next day and found pieces of a white bed sheet hanging in the barbed wire fence behind the church.

A salesman rang his doorbell and tried to push his way inside the house. Warren said, "Let's see if I can find Old Betsy here behind the door." The salesman ran to his car, jumped in and burned rubber up the road as Warren fired his shotgun into the air.

Later the same day, Warren stopped by to see our brother Curtis and while they were sitting on the front porch, the same salesman came down the driveway in his car. He stopped, got out, saw Warren and said, "I think I'm at the wrong house." Warren ran to his own car, got his pistol and shot into the air again as the salesman burned more rubber up the driveway. Warren told Curtis, "Pa 'taught his sons well."

From early childhood, Warren's main topic of conversation was automobiles and his saying was known to all, "Warren's the name and Chevy's the game." (Until he died in 2002, he still threatened to "plant" people in his own private boot hill, including me.)

Our home no longer stands on Banjo Lane, but will always be there in memory: our safe haven from the storm, where young hunters and fishers came back to when tired and wounded, at the end of the day. No matter how far we roamed or how long we were gone, we knew a light would be shining in the window, supper would be ready and the house would be warm.

When warm and fed, we read by the light of an oil lamp and traveled the world in books from the school library. With rain pouring on the tin roof for a lullaby, we went to dreamland and slept the whole night through.

Part 3

Our son Mike and Pa at home on Banjo Lane. 1970

Polaroid Christmas Eve on Banjo Lane (1972) Bobbie, Warren and Eldridge (El)

Chapter 7

Kermit and Elizabeth Easter

Kermit and Elizabeth Easter (Pa and Mama) at home on Banjo Lane. 1965

My dad, Kermit Easter, (Pa) the youngest of George and Alice Berrier Easter's four children, was born November 17, 1909 and like his dad, became a one-horse farmer on Stewart's Creek. His only public job was in the 1930s, when he "hired out" for a few days on the new Beamer Bridge on Highway 89. As he said it, "Never had much to do with none a' that boss man stuff."

We almost never had money until we sold tobacco in fall and when things got up tight, Pa sold locust fence posts and pulpwood and repaired barbed wire fences for H V Holder. He was also known to brew up a batch of moonshine on backwoods branch banks. That too was hard work, but easier than plowing all day with a bull tongue plow and sawing wood with a crosscut saw.

His best friend was the Iver Johnson shotgun he used to hunt squirrels, rabbits and chase stray animals out of the garden. When neighbors celebrated Christmas with firecrackers, Pa celebrated with the shotgun and he and Mama often settled an argument with it; then he slept with it.

To my knowledge, none of my ancestors had ever taken a vacation from the nose-to-grindstone effort of red-dirt farming. Pa broke the mold when he began taking "a little time off." He didn't say where or why he was going; he just went, came back a day or two later and went back to work as if nothing had happened.

He never "went in much" for housework, but his meals had better be on the table at the right time. His place was at the head of the table and nobody had enough nerve to "set in my cheer." Mama once failed to break his bread at supper. (Instead of slicing or cutting pone bread with a knife, we broke pieces off by hand.) He told her in no uncertain terms, "It'll be a sad day in Hell when I break my own bread."

That's how it was on Stewart's Creek: man was King of his Castle and did no house work, because he already had all he could do running the farm and shooting the shotgun. When it came time to work in the fields, that was a different story; "everybody better be there helping or there'd be 'you know what' to pay."

Pa's everyday outfit was an old floppy hat, brogans, patched "bib" overalls and a long-sleeved shirt. He carried his pocket watch (with chain attached) in a bib pocket and his billfold in another beside it. With money hard to come by, he dreaded spending the little he had and when it came time to pay, his hand almost got tangled up in the watch chain. (Warren and I stood by, just in case he needed rescuing.) In all fairness, money was scarce around our house until we sold some 'baccer, ivy or likker.' Sometimes, we had none at all.

Pa and Mama didn't exactly agree on certain things, in fact, most things. They never actually got to "fist city," but often held heated discussions of each other's ignorant parents, kinfolks and ancestors. I learned early on that my family tree was a total disaster on both sides of the fence and it was a wonder I ever got here.

Grandma did the quarreling at their house and Grandpa didn't hang around any more than he had to. He either took refuge in the tack room or let off steam by chasing chickens around the smoke house. When he couldn't escape, he just sat and listened because he'd heard it all before.

The biggest reason for owning a shotgun or rifle was to put "food on the eatin' table:" such as rabbits, squirrels and bobwhites and even the poorest of families owned a shotgun. Younger boys and some younger girls carried a slingshot and a pocket full of rocks, but when they grew up, they too hunted with a real weapon.

"Old Betsy." (After a "small war" on the front porch.)

Pa's best friend was "Old Betsy" and a bureau drawer full of shells stayed on stand-by at all times: in case some varmint "needed a little lead in its hide." It helped him bring home the bacon, it guarded the still place, protected the cornfields from crows and saved the garden from a "whole damn bunch a' them varmints." It kept us safe from outlaws; bad guys, "suck-egg" dogs and he sometimes shot into the air just for the heck it.

During one of my parent's mini-wars, Old Betsy wound up with a broken stock. (See tape in photo above.) After another all-out free-for-all, Pa headed for the Graveyard Road with the shotgun and a double hand-full of shells and told us, "If you smell anything stinkin' out yonder, it'll be me." Just thinking about the graveyard and the shotgun together scared me half to death. I did wonder how many shells it took to shoot your self. I waited, worried and listened, but heard no gunshots and he soon came back home safe and sound. I never knew who won the war that day.

When a neighbor and his wife had an argument, he told her he was going to shoot himself and went into the barn with his shotgun. She heard a shot and a few minutes later, she heard another and wondered if he'd missed the first time. Before very long, he came back home, hung up the shotgun and lived to be an old man.

Pa and Mama had friends in for a Saturday night shindig and everything was going great guns until Mama decided to wind a bucket of water from the well. When the bucket settled down into the water and gave its usual tug, she thought somebody was in the well and had a screaming fit that scared everybody witless. They raced around like a chicken with its head cut off until somebody held a head count. When they found nobody missing, they decided nobody was in the well and my cold chills finally calmed down. (I still wondered if anybody was in the well.)

According to my younger brothers, the family wars became more physical after Warren and I left home. They often hid under the bed to avoid getting hit by flying crockery and hid the shotgun, because the parent who got it first began shooting. During one particular war, Pa shot the warming closet off the back of the cook stove and when Grandma came by, she asked what happened to the stove. I don't know what he told her, but I know for a fact: Pa never cleaned house when I was growing up. Apparently, he began doing so in later years and did it with the shotgun.

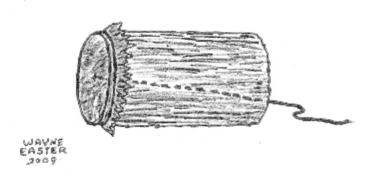

Dumb Bull

In his younger days, Pa made a Dumb Bull from a foot-long piece of hollow log: with a banjo-head cover tied tightly over one end. He fastened a heavy bees-wax covered string to the inside center of the cover and fed it out the open end of the log. When he reached inside and pulled his fingers along the string, it made a racket, as he told it, "Like you ain't never seen before."

While walking along the Cleve Thomas Road one day, he heard some people talking up on Gardner's Ridge. According to him, they were "not from our parts" and had "sneaked in breaking ivy." (No landowner cared who broke his ivy and come November, everybody just headed for the woods with fertilizer sacks to make some extra money.)

Maybe Pa was having a bad day, or maybe he was bored, or maybe he saw a chance to try out his new toy. When he heard the people, he ran home, got his dumb bull and hurried along Gardner's Ridge. He sneaked in behind some bushes where two strangers were happily going about the business of breaking ivy; with no idea anyone else was within a mile.

Again as he told it, "I reached inside and give that string a dry yank and one of 'em said, "Listen." I give 'er a bigger yank and all Hell broke loose. They climbed all over the ivy bushes and the laurels and each other and everything else that got in the way. Ivy sacks be-damned, they run and fell straight down through the bluff and I kept yankin' the string and thrashin' the bushes."

"They run through the branch at the bottom of the hill, crossed the Cleve Thomas Road and run up through the pasture: might-near afraid to look back. Last I seen, they was a' headin' out a' sight towards Lambsburg." (That may have been the reason few people prowled in the bluffs when I was growing up. After hearing his story, I was leery of going near them myself.

Mama, (Elizabeth Whitaker Easter) one of Bob and Molly Wood Whitaker's thirteen children, was born May 29, 1916 in Surry County. She was "schooled" (in a one-room school house) and made us go to school under threat of bodily harm. As she said it, "Get on that bus and try to learn something or you gonna' grow up dumb just like your daddy."

She was the driving force in raising her five boys and tried to keep us clean, clothed, fed, unhurt *and* schooled. Considering how rough we worked and played, she had her hands full. In the early years, she worked in the fields with the rest of the family, kept the household going, canned food for winter and cooked three meals every day of the year. In later years she told us there were times when we had very little to eat for the next meal. The variety was often limited, but mealtimes always came.

She was a cook without equal and the squirrels we brought home became feasts to write home about. We skinned them, singed off any hair sticking to the body with a burning newspaper and she transformed them into squirrel dumplings that were almost as good as fried chicken. (When we found a shotgun pellet in a piece of squirrel, we just removed it and kept eating. Nothing, but absolutely nothing got in the way of Mama's squirrel dumplings.)

When we caught a 'possum, Pa fed it corn and other "clean foods" for a few days to "fatten it up." When we were ready to eat it, he killed it with a hammer blow to the head and Mama dipped it in the washtub of boiling water to scald it so the hair would come off. That worked just fine until the day she dipped one in the tub that crawled back out and ran into the woods. She vowed she would never clean another one and true to her word, we ate no more 'possums.

Mama's skills were unlimited and except for a few minor things like plowing and hunting, she could shoot the shotgun and saw down trees with the best. When she and Pa held one of their mini-wars and she got the shotgun first, she blazed away. The discussions of our ancestors then came to a screeching halt and Pa stayed out of the way: far away. Before very long, everything got back to normal, at least what passed for normal on our hill.

She was Doctor Mama, who fixed sore toes, bad colds, bee stings, poison ivy and settled major disputes among brothers. She swung a mean hickory switch and the few whippings she gave us were well deserved. What worked best was that certain look she had; without her saying a single word, we knew what to do. When her ears began smoking, it was "Look out, Louise" and we headed for the hills. (Again, before very long, everything got back to normal.)

One very bad year, we ran out of everything at the same time and Mama began working in the mills in Mount Airy. She worked there five days a week and still cooked the meals, washed and mended clothes, canned food for winter and did a hundred other things. Like every other woman on Stewart's Creek, she did what had to be done and then some.

The Easter clan had harvested corn exactly the same way ever since Moses came over on the Mayflower. They pulled the corn ears off the stalks and threw them into piles on the ground, came back later, threw them into the wagon and hauled them home, just like God intended.

Mama went down in Stewart's Creek history when she figured out how to save some extra work. She suggested they bring the horse and wagon along and throw the ears of corn directly into the wagon instead of on the ground. Grandpa said the wagon would tear down the cornstalks. She told him the stalks would soon be ploughed down anyway and before very long, they pulled the corn ears off, threw them directly into the wagon and saved an extra handling of the corn. Mama said Grandma never got over it.

When Mama was young, a full eclipse of the sun brought the world to an end at their house. It got dark in the middle of the day, the chickens went to roost and the birds quit singing. Her mama (Grandma Whitaker) told them, "Lordy mercy, young'uns, the world's comin' to a' end and Pa ain't here. What're we gonna' do"

Grandma Whitaker told a tale of two frogs that fell into a churn of milk waiting to be churned. One frog splashed around a while, then gave up and drowned. The other frog kept swimming and next morning, it was still alive: sitting on top of the butter it had churned. Mama told us the same tale and said, "When the going gets rough, you go churn you some butter."

Just like the Easters, the Whitakers were "all eat up with smarts." Mama's sister once hired a taxi to a Mr. Dowdy's house, where she hadn't been before. When the taxi stopped, she went to the house, talked to someone, got back in the taxi and told the driver, "Mr. Dowdy don't live here." The driver said, "I know, I just stopped for that red light."

At left: Grandma and Grandpa Whitaker. (Molly and Bob) At right: in back, their sons, Luther and Curtis and in front, Claude and Robert: with Grandpa Whitaker on the steps at right. (Made at Slate Mountain about 1940.)

According to an 1880 census, Grandpa Whitaker was born June 1, 1876 and Grandma was born February 11, 1884: both in Surry County. Their first child died, but the twelve others were: Lillie, Bill, Carlyle, Etta, Woodrow, Elizabeth, Luther, Curtis, Robert, Eliza, Claude, and Gladys: not necessarily in that order.

I never knew Grandpa and Grandma Whitaker as well as Pa's parents, because they lived on the other side of the county. They never owned a house or land and sharecropped all their working years. In the late 1930s, we spent the night with them in the cabin shown below.

My grandparent's home near Westfield N C. (Late 1930s)

All their years were hard, but the worst one came when a landowner kept their share of a tobacco crop they grew on his farm; Mama said they had very little to eat that winter. Her brothers threatened to burn the landowner's buildings, but Grandpa said no.

After Grandma Whitaker died, (June 19, 1958) Grandpa stayed with Pa and Mama on occasion and I remember him making splints from poplar trees to "bottom" chairs. He died March 24, 1979 at well over a hundred years of age.

Some people were "sot in their ways" and had no desire for an automobile. "You ever seen a horse or a mule git stuck in a mud hole? If the Lord had a' meant us to ride, He'd a' put tires on us." (The biggest reason *we* didn't own one was the fact that it took a whole lot of what we had the least of: money.)

When Pa was in his teens, he bought a T-Model Ford and gave Grandma Easter (his mom) a ride. The steering wheel came off, they ran out of the road into a cornfield and she never rode with him again. He only had the car for a short time and didn't own another until 1948 when I was 16 years old.

Grover and Etta Thomas (Mama's sister) and family often came to visit in their 1930s black Chevrolet. When ready to go home, Grover said, "O k everybody, get in the car." The last kid to get in was "it" and the race was on. When everybody was on-board, they left in a cloud of dust: as Warren, the dog and I chased along behind. I hoped and prayed we'd have a car like that someday.

I'd never tried to drive until Bill Freeman told me take his 1932 Ford coupe for a spin: alone. All the pedals and gadgets had their own ideas about how things worked and after killing the engine several times, I finally loped it out to the barn, but won no driving awards that day.

When Pa bought our first car, (an A-Model coupe) we finally had some transportation besides the horse and we were right up there in the thick of things. Another of his famous sayings then came into being, "You can take a stick 'a stove wood, a pair a' pliers, a piece a' balin' wire and a drink a' likker' and make a' A Model." (We had the first and last of those items on hand at all times.)

On a 1948 Saturday, I was trying-out my brand new driver's license, as Pa and I headed to Lambsburg in the A-Model. I was doing a first-rate job until we met an almost new Ford coupe directly in front of Rosssie Golding's Mill: running so fast it was hard to believe it could stay in the road. While watching it out the back window, I wandered over on the left side of the road. Just as I got stopped, another car came along going just as fast as the first one. Pa almost had a spasm and when it ran out of the road and crashed under Rossie's woodpile, I actually had one.

A Blue Ridge Parkway Ranger crawled out of the wreck, slapped his hat on the ground and said, "Why in the name of heaven don't you stay on your side of the road?" I told him we had just about got "run-over" and was about out of control. He said that was probably true and told us he was chasing a Lowe man who was hauling a load of liquor. Some weeks later, a letter came in the mail stating that someone in North Wilkesboro had paid to have the Ranger's Pontiac repaired.

On another day to remember, Pa let me drive the A Model to Beulah School all by myself: the only day in twelve years I didn't ride the bus. I'd always known that sooner or later, I'd get it all together and sooner had arrived.

One bright sunny morning, the famous race car driver, Speedy Easter chic-a-lacked down Pine Ridge Road in his 1931 A Model Ford coupe in a cloud of dust. A great smell of burning motor oil boiled up through the floorboards and a little steam spewed from the radiator cap. I was King of the Highway with a powerhouse under the hood and everybody I met was my friend, because everybody waved back.

The best part of all was when I drove into the school parking lot while all the girls watched. Mr. Important had arrived, had a set of wheels and was six feet tall, at least. It was a feeling everybody should have at least once in a lifetime. I don't remember much about classes that day, but it was one heck of a day and all too soon, it came to an end. I made it back home with the fenders intact and Pa breathed a huge sigh of relief. It was my greatest ride.

One December day, Pa had me drive Guy Haunn and I-Joe "Dannel" (Daniel) to a house on Haystack Road to buy some "Christmas Likker." On the way back, they sampled the merchandise, sang a while, drank a while and were having a great time. While going uphill above Walter Marshall's tobacco barn, they got into an argument and told me to stop so they could get out and have a little pow-wow right in the middle of the road. I tried to drive on to the top of the hill, but I-Joe pulled the choke lever all the way out and killed the engine. They got out, had a loud discussion in the middle of the road, became friends again, got back in the car and we went on up the hill.

Pa and some friends were riding around one Sunday, sampling a jug and having a good time, when a tire went flat. They removed the inner tube, found no leak, pumped it back up with the hand pump and went on their way. It soon went flat again with the same results.

When they removed the inner tube for the third time and pumped it up, they still found no leak. Somebody stabbed the tube with his pocketknife, they patched the hole, put the inner tube back in, pumped the tire up once more and it didn't go flat anymore.

Every car owner bragged about how good his climbed a hill and "all that power she's got under that hood." When asked about his jalopy, one proud soul said, "I'll put 'er up against anybody's anytime, anywhere. That thing hauled me and Missy and a gallon of buttermilk up the Isom Surratt hill in high gear, by crackity. Another time, I give 'er a good running start and topped Bate's Hill in high gear too."

Our unpaved country roads were just fine in summer, but Pa drove all year like he was hauling eggs. He drove into a curve one day doing maybe fifteen miles per hour, when some gravel rattled under a fender. He looked over at me and said, "Son, if I hadn't a gagged 'er there, she'd a went over in spite of me." I almost got double lockjaw, trying to look impressed and not smile.

His driving ability, which was never great, got worse as he got older and everybody who met him stayed ready for anything. He once turned left in front of another vehicle near Mt. Airy and almost caused a wreck. He told Mama, "Looks like he would'a seen me."

Someone told about driving west on Highway 89 in a long line of slow-moving traffic, with nowhere to pass on the two-lane road. He guessed who might be leading the pack and sure enough, a few cars turned off and he saw Kermit Easter up-front, getting it done at twenty miles per hour. A deputy sheriff (N A "Bill" Lowe) told me to tell Pa that if he didn't stop driving drunk, he'd be forced to arrest him.

In the 1960s, Helen and I made a home movie of Pa spinning and sliding on the snowy hillside above Walter Marshall's tobacco barn. He was about "two sheets in the wind," but thanks to the pickup "being trained," he kept it in the road and when he turned onto Banjo Lane, the deep ruts almost led him home.

Pa quit the "heavy farming" when the first Social Security check came in the mail and leased his tobacco allotment to others. Except for growing and selling tomatoes, he became a man of leisure. "All that money" was a like a gift from the Gods and he was never broke again.

With his "seegar," a little snort and a daily trip to Crooked Oak Grocery, his day was made. He and his cronies sat around "down at the store," smoked, chewed, spit, poured salted peanuts in "little bottle Co' Colers" and solved all the world's problems.

In 1982, Mama became afraid to ride with him and (at age 66) got her own driver's license, bought a Pinto automobile and hit the roads. According to my journal, she drove the twelve miles to our house for the first time on January 30, 1983. When she pulled into our driveway, I decided once again, I hadn't yet seen it all.

As Pa got older, he spent more and more time in his favorite chair: daydreaming about the good old days and wondering when supper would be ready. In warm weather, he sat on the front porch or in the yard under a shade tree. In cold weather, he sat inside, as close to the heater as possible and "fired 'er as hot as she'll run."

By then, his biggest worry was having enough firewood to stay warm all winter and Warren, Curtis, El and I made sure he never ran out; we sawed and split, while he rested on a log at the woodpile. Since they lived close by, my brothers did most of the woodcutting.

Until the last few weeks of his life, he and Mama held daily discussions of each other's ancestors, personal faults and downfalls. There were many and even after fifty plus years, they kept coming up with new stuff. Like the radio and t v, their volume was always loud, but got louder as they got older. (They also didn't hear as well as they once did.)

For many years, family tradition brought all of the family back to the home place on Christmas Eve to exchange gifts and eat a big meal. No one knew it at the time, but 1983 was Pa's last. He became sick and died February 9, 1984.

Mama's new trailer and her Pinto (at the right.) (1985)

A year later, Mama sold the Banjo Lane home place and bought back an acre of land at the foot of Jim's Knob, which they had sold to Crissie Smith in earlier years. She said the old place was too far from the main road and she didn't want to live there any longer: especially by herself. She bought a new house trailer (seen above) and "moved up on the road," as she'd always wanted to do. (Some of my childhood ambitions were to become rich and famous and build my parents a new house. As it came to be, I did none of those and Mama bought her own house.)

She no longer had to worry about the big mud hole and the muddy hillside in winter, or staying warm in the worn-out drafty house. By living "up on the road", she could "watch all them cars go by and see people sometimes."

My younger brothers Curtis and El helped her set up housekeeping beside a log wine barn Jim Smith built in the early 1900s. The new house had an automatic electric furnace but she had them build an extra room on the back and install a wood heater so she could have a wood fire "like people are supposed to have."

As Carrie Smith had done some 50 years earlier, Mama soon had flowers and vegetables growing in every square inch of available space. Just like back at the old place, she kept a big supply of food on hand. "Who wants to run the store for every little thing?"

For the next 20 years, she canned and froze food for winter and cooked the big meals on weekends and holidays. As her health declined, she quit the "big cooking" and as of now, (2009) grandchildren and great grandchildren do the big cooking.

After twenty plus years in the trailer, thanks to my brothers who keep her supplied with wood, she still keeps a wood fire burning in winter. The electric furnace would be easier to use, but she still fires the wood stove and keeps flashlights, oil lamps and candles ready at all times, "Just in case the power goes out." Just like back at the home place on Banjo Lane, an up-to-date copy of Blum's almanac hangs on the wall. "How in the world is anybody gonna' know how to do anything without a Blum's Almanac?"

Pa

Mama

Mama and Pa at the home place on Banjo Lane (1971)

Pa, Mama, Wayne and Warren (1930s)

Eldridge, Curtis and our second car, an A-Model sedan (Late 1940s)

(Footnote: Mama died January 16, 2013 at age 96.)

Chapter 8

George And Alice Easter

My first known ancestor in the new world, Michael Easter, came from Holland in the 1700s and settled near the town of Welcome in Davidson/Rowan County, N C. He became sick in 1783 and made a will that described his property and how he wanted it divided.

In 1827, one of his descendants, David Easter, moved to the foot of Sugar Loaf Mountain in Carroll County, Virginia. He was the first of what became my many kin people in that area. (As of today, you can't throw a rock in the Flower Gap area without hitting an Easter.)

George and Alice Easter

My grandfather, George Washington Easter was born April 15, 1878 and my grandmother, Alice Berrier Easter was born July 13, 1878: both in the Flower Gap area of Carroll County. They were married April 20, 1899, bought a tract of land in Surry County, N C and moved there around the turn of the century.

They built a one-room log cabin in a valley beside a small stream: a half-mile west of Stewart's Creek and other than attending Crooked Oak Primitive Baptist Church and family re-unions, they seldom traveled and the farm became their whole life.

Their four children, in order of birth were, Grace, Manuel, Maude and Kermit. Grace married Ed Smith and they owned a farm on Old Low Gap Road. (Maple Grove Church Road today.) Manuel and his wife Kate lived in Galax, Virginia, then moved to Oregon. He was the only one of the four children who moved out of Surry County. Maude married Allen Seal and they too owned a farm on Old Low Gap Road.

Kermit (my dad and the youngest) married Elizabeth Whitaker and they too became farmers on Stewart's Creek. In the beginning, they depended heavily on my grandparents, their horse, wagon, plows, tobacco barns and tobacco pack house. When Pa finally bought a horse, we began a long climb out of the deep hole we started in.

We continued helping my grandparents and using their tobacco barns and wagon until Grandpa died in 1947. Grandma then sold the farm at auction and we were forced to build our own tobacco barn: just one of many changes we made at that time.

Their log cabin had a white oak shingle roof, a single door and no windows. Some early cabins had holes in the walls with "shutters" (covers) that could be opened and closed for air and light, but theirs had none and it was dark inside, even in the middle of the day.

The Smoke House

A good-luck horseshoe hung over the door, with the ends turned up to catch all the luck that came by. The door itself was made of rough-planks, held shut with a latch and string and was never locked. When the rock and mud chimney was moved to their new frame house, the hole left behind was covered with planks. (Seen on the left end above.) The cabin then became the Smoke House, where they smoked and stored meat.

Grandpa stored his auger, fro, spare horseshoes, plow points, pig wringers, crosscut saw and plow wrenches inside, along with his wine kegs that sat on a low shelf. He made wine (for medicinal purposes) and furnished "Communion Wine" for meetings at Zion Hill Primitive Baptist Church. (Established July 1878. Local people called it "Crooked Oak Church.")

Grandpa didn't care much for church, but he always went with Grandma on Meeting Day. She was a devoted member and sang the loudest and highest of all. When she sang one Foot-washing Day, a dog howled outside, then all the kids howled, then everybody laughed.

If a traveling preacher happened to spend the night, Grandma fed him fried chicken and let him sleep in the feather bed. Grandpa let him test the Communion Wine and it was a known fact that Primitive Baptist Preachers knew good wine when they saw it. After some extensive taste tests, Grandpa's wine always passed with flying colors and the happy preacher went to dreamland and slept the night away in Grandma's feather bed. (It was enough to make me want to be a preacher.) On occasion, Grandpa gave a lucky friend a cup of wine and very special friends got two. He gave me a drink one day that made my legs weak and warmed me all the way to my toes.

He sometimes chased chickens around the smoke house. Maybe they didn't lay enough eggs or maybe he was just letting off steam or maybe he was mad at Grandma or maybe Grandma was mad at him. Whatever the case, he could move when chasing chickens.

They gathered eggs every day from a row of straw-filled nests under a back shelter at the smoke house. Two of the nests had porcelain nest eggs, which made no sense, because *our* chickens laid eggs just fine without a pattern.

One day when the signs were right, he and I made white oak shingles. (If not made in the right sign, they curled up when nailed on the roof.) It was slow demanding work, but he was patient and using his fro and wooden mallet, he made a huge pile. We stacked them high and placed heavy rocks on top prevent warping while they dried.

He may have been the last shingle maker on Stewart's Creek, because I never saw anyone else make them. Tin eventually replaced wood shingles, which was easier and faster to install, didn't warp, didn't leak, never needed replacing and "outlasted you if you died when you ought to."

We made cider one fall day, as he turned the handle and I fed apples into the mill. The apples were ground into a mush and the juice came out into a bucket. When yellow jackets fell in the juice, he just dipped them out and we kept on grinding. He fed the mush to the hog, strained the juice through a cloth and poured it into jugs to become cider and vinegar. He also pressed grapes in the mill to make wine and jelly.

The New House

The "New House" (already old when I was young) stood near the smokehouse. It had a tin roof, unpainted weatherboard siding on the outside and beaded ceiling inside. A four-pane window on the west wall of the kitchen looked out on the smokehouse and garden. The rock and mud chimney that was moved from the smoke house had settled over the years and leaned so far from the wall, it looked like it would fall, but it never did.

I warmed by the roaring fireplace on cold rainy days, one side at a time, as steam came off my clothes. Grandpa popped homegrown popcorn in a wire screen popper over the fire and told me, "Them popping sounds in the fire means it's gonna' snow, boy." A backlog burned continually until bedtime, when he "banked" it with hot ashes to help re-start the fire next morning. Grandma once cooked complete meals in the fireplace and even in my time, she baked corn bread in a Dutch oven buried in the hot ashes. She saved the old ashes for fertilizer and to make lye soap.

Grandma's cats lived under the kitchen porch (seen above) and when they saw me coming, they headed for the hills. They were "all eat up" with fleas that ate me up and when one bit me, it made a place as big as fifty cents that itched bad enough to tear the hide off. For that very reason, cats and dogs were never my best friends.

A water bucket sat on the porch shelf, with a dipper to drink from. Nobody worried about who drank from what; everybody just drank from the same dipper. That was also true of water jugs carried to the fields. When about to die in the hot summer sun, nobody worried about where the water came from, who drank it from what, or how hot it was; they just drank it, kept on living and pretty soon, they drank some more.

When Grandpa peeled an apple, he sliced it, ate it and got a dipper of water from the bucket. He rinsed his mouth, poured water over his false teeth and put them back in his mouth. He did the same after meals and many years later I learned why.

Muddy shoes and dirty work-clothes were parked on the kitchen porch and strings of leather britches (air-dried green beans) and dried red peppers hung from the rafters. The peppers were used as seasoning for home made sausage and it only took one taste to learn why they were called "hot" peppers. A gallon of water later, my mouth almost cooled back to normal. Only then was I told, "Them things'll set a broom straw field on fire, boy."

Screens on the doors and windows kept most of the flies outside, but for any that got inside, "pull-down sticker" flytraps and a fly swatter kept them partly under control. "When you see that screen door covered with flies tryin' to get in, you'll know it's gonna' rain." We had no screens at our house in the early years and it was "open-house" for every flying varmint in the state of Georgia. We lived with fly swatters in hand, but were always outnumbered.

Grandpa and Grandma lived, ate and slept in the only heated room, the kitchen. Their straw-tick bed sat in one corner and the kitchen table, chairs and a bench sat under the north-wall window. A white enameled wood cook stove sat in another corner: with a warming closet and a hot water tank. A tin-door pie safe in still another corner had pies in it that I could smell a mile away. We too had a pie safe, but our pies never made it out of the kitchen. Sometimes, the Gods smiled and Grandma gave me a slice.

When I churned butter for her, she told me every time, "Don't churn too hard or you'll slop the milk out." Like Mama, she was a busy person, but with one important difference: she didn't shoot the shotgun. Most women were afraid of guns, but Mama was afraid of nothing. When she and Pa had one of their mini-wars and she got the shotgun first, she held her own target practice, while Pa found other things to do in other places, far away places.

A hand-cranked-telephone on the kitchen wall was once part of a party-line system. The wires were long-gone, but the white chestnut telephone poles (with green glass insulators) still stood in a row along the Cleve Thomas Road.

Each home had it's own series of long and short rings that were generated by cranking the phone handle for different lengths of time. All phones rang at the same time and by the different series of rings, everybody knew who was being called. Nobody *ever,* for God's sake, *never* listened to other people's calls, so help us Lord.

Grandpa could forecast the weather by checking the sundogs that came up in the western sky. He could tell by the thickness of corn shucks and how black the caterpillars were how bad the winter would be. (I learned right off: when the sky turned black over Fisher's Peak and thunder began, a thunderstorm was coming for sure and when I saw snow come over the top in winter, I could predict snow in the immediate future, almost always, maybe.)

A Kasco's Feed and Seed Store calendar hung on the kitchen wall that advertised Raymond's Little Liver Pills and Cardui, (a medicine with a high alcohol content for ailing women.) It told when the sun would rise and set and what phase the moon was in and had small fish symbols for each day that showed which day the fish would bite best: the blacker the fish, the better the day to go fishing.

Best of all was the Blum's Almanac that hung beside it and it took a genius to understand everything in it. It was the farmer's Bible and absolutely nothing could be done without checking the Zodiac signs. It told which part of the body they were in on a given day, when to sow, plant, plow, cut fire wood and timber, make and install wooden shingles, de-horn calves, castrate pigs, harvest crops, re-shoe horses, pull teeth and go fishing. Woe unto anybody who planted potatoes or "shoed" horses in the wrong moon sign.

Some of the big words were way over my head, but I didn't ask for help, because world-famous scouts and explorers, such as a certain person, just didn't go around telling everybody what they didn't understand.

Blum's Almanac: 167th edition.

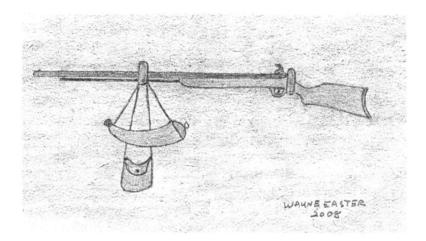

Grandpa's Muzzleloader

Grandpa's muzzleloader hung high on the wall, along with a ramrod, a small leather bag of bullets, wadding and a cow horn full of gunpowder. It hadn't been fired in years, but he once hunted squirrels, rabbits and wild turkeys and killed the hog with it.

Down one step from the kitchen was the "settin' room," (sitting room) with an ancient settee covered in cracked black leather. It sat under the front-porch window and the finest bed of all time sat in a corner: the "Company Bed." It had a feather-filled tick and was only used for important company, like Primitive Baptist Preachers. (I wondered what it would be like to sleep in such a soft bed and when Grandpa died in 1947, I stayed with Grandma that summer and slept in it.)

A kerosene lamp, with an always-clean glass globe, (also reserved for important company) sat on the fireplace mantel and a pedal sewing machine stood beside the fireplace. The settin' room chimney was made of bricks and didn't lean away from the house like the kitchen chimney. The fireplace, like the whole room, was also reserved for important company.

Old faded photographs of Easter and Berrier ancestors frowned down from dark oval frames on the settin' room wall. They glared at me like I'd done something wrong and even if I had, how in tarnation could they know about it? Their eyes followed me every time I walked by, but I got even; I glared back.

A boxed-in stairway led to two upstairs bedrooms piled high with books and magazines. I sat by a window on the south end and read some great stories from the 1920s and '30's and now wish I'd kept some of the better ones. The window also gave a great eye-level view of the Big John Apple tree downhill beside the spring path.

Another bedroom joined the downstairs settin' room: with a bed, dresser, wardrobe and a permanent smell of cured tobacco from the basement below. We hung sticks of tobacco there to dampen so they could be handled without crumbling. We then sorted the tobacco into different grades, tied it into "hands," (bunches) bundled it into large sacks and sold it on the tobacco market in Mount Airy. Grandma also stored canned stuff, potatoes, apples, cabbage and turnips there in winter. By spring of the year, the leftover potatoes had foot-long sprouts and the leftover apples were shriveled and dried. She grew flowers beside the basement door, using seeds saved from last year's flowers.

Hornets and wasper's (wasps) built nests up under the house eaves in summer and in late fall, they flew all around the house: searching for a place to winter over. I hoped they and everything else that had a stinger didn't make it 'til spring.

A front yard tree grew pears that were life threatening, rock-hard, fell like a brick, never mellowed and didn't taste good either: something that almost never happened in my world. "Why even grow a pear that could fall on you and kill you, when you couldn't eat it.

A six-foot high by six-foot wide boxwood bush grew in the back yard, along with a purple blooming lily of the valley tree. Thanks to Grandpa's grafting, an apple tree beside the kitchen grew two different kinds of apples. When the yard grass got too high, they "stobbed" the cow there to save pushing the reel mower all over creation. I tried mowing with the man-killer once and found out right away, it was harder than sawing dry wood with a dull crosscut saw.

The Big John Apple tree beside the spring path had been there about as long as the smokehouse. Grandpa once fell out of it while picking apples and landed on his feet. I climbed it every chance I got and was warned, "Don't you fall, boy." While climbing near the top in 1948, I saw the new fire tower on Fisher's Peak for the first time.

We ate cherries in a huge tree beside the path: as high as we dared to climb and played in a nearby blackberry thicket, until we were told to "stay out of there." We were playing there another day and were told again in no uncertain terms, "Get the blankety blank out of there and stay out of there," When we learned that was where Grandma emptied the chamber pot, we "stayed out of there."

The spring path had worn deep from carrying water along it for so many years. It led downhill by the John Apple tree, crossed a plank foot log over the branch and continued to the spring that came from under a north-facing bluff. The high bluff blocked the low-in-the-sky winter sun and snow hung around the spring for weeks.

The spring branch ran under a walk-in springhouse that had green moss on the walls and roof and no matter how hot the weather in summer, it stayed cool inside. Spring lizards and toad frogs lived there and Grandpa kept watermelons and mush melons cooling in the water, ever ready for tobacco primings, Sunday company and other drastic emergencies such as perishing grandchildren. He also kept his herb-bitters cooling there and they tasted so bad, nobody had enough nerve to go near them.

An August 1940 hurricane brought what became known as the "Forty Flood" and Stewart's Creek backed up a half mile, almost to the springhouse. It was hard to believe there was that much water in the whole world. It was the biggest flood "anybody ever seen, even bigger than "that'n' in 1916," as the old timers said it. All bottomland crops were destroyed, but most bottom owners also had fields on the high ridges, so nobody had a total loss. When the creek went back to normal, everything was covered with mud. (When Watershed Lake was built in the 1970s, Stewart's Creek once again backed up to the springhouse and stayed.)

My grandparent's only varmint-proof place for growing food was their fenced-in "good" garden beside the smoke house. They grew beans, corn, peas and tomatoes by the ton and best of all: they grew strawberries, gooseberries and grapes. They "followed" the signs, which always worked, most of the time. When a late freeze wiped out early plantings, Grandma told Grandpa, "I told you the almanac said it was too early, but you wouldn't listen, you old goat" Grandpa didn't say anything.

A small hill some fifteen feet high and thirty feet long stood beside the garden and having found arrowheads in the creek bottoms, I was already an Indian expert and knew it was an Indian Mound. I could almost smell the gold, pottery, tomahawks and other magical stuff buried there and made big plans to dig it out.

Then I read about the hexes and curses some sacred places had on them and chickened out. I wasn't exactly the brightest chip on the old block, but I had more sense than to dig in there and get myself all hexed up. So it was until Tom Senter bought Grandpa's farm in late 1947. When he had the mound pushed down, not even an arrowhead was found and another of my great Indian theories went down in flames.

Grandpa kept bee gums under his grapevines that I stayed far away from, because every bee in the country had my name on it's stinger: just waiting to nail me. He had no fear at all of any kind of bee and waded right in like they were no more than a bunch of flies.

Grandma dried bunches of a good smelling plant called Pennyroyal that made the house smell good. It grew wild in the hillside pasture and she made tea from the peppermint she picked along the branch banks. On top of that, she was Doctor Grandma.

With the nearest doctor "plumb over the mountain," people in our world figured they'd die before he got around. For that very reason, Grandma and everybody else kept remedies on hand that would cure any ailment known to mankind. They gathered herbs and roots from the woods and fields and some tasted so bad they curled your toes.

They also bought stuff by mail or from traveling snake-oil salesmen and woe unto the family that didn't keep Carter's Little Liver Pills, Rosebud Salve, Mercurochrome, Iodine and Black Draught on hand at all times. The worst thing about Black Draught: it was the worst tasting stuff on Earth and us kids had to take it, whether we were sick or not. Who ever heard of somebody having to take medicine when they felt good?

Grandpa's herb bitters probably worked for him, because he was never sick. The biggest reason being, no self-respecting malady would come within five miles of it. He gathered certain wild herbs from the woods, mixed them with water and kept a quart jar full cooling in the springhouse. He passed by every now and then and got a little snort. One day, when nobody was looking, I too got a little snort and it tasted so bad I was almost afraid to look at it again. How in the world could anybody drink anything that tasted that bad?

A jar of moonshine stayed on standby in some homes: ever ready to fight off chigger bites, snakebites, frostbites and bad weather. It was said some people had bad weather all year and got "frost bit' in summer and "snake bit" in winter.

My brother Warren and I would never have grown up without the magical qualities of Mercurochrome and Iodine. When painted on a hurt place, the big red smear became a badge of honor; the bigger the smear, the better it looked and the worse people thought we'd been hurt. If you had no skinned knees and stubbed toes painted bright red, you were a sissy, a fraidy cat, a Mama's boy or some other kind of freak.

The Easter clan had harvested corn exactly the same way since the beginning of time: they hauled it home in the wagon and piled it in the middle of the road and there it stayed until corn-shucking day. That was how Grandpa did it and so did we; when a car, wagon or horseback rider came along, they had to detour around a huge pile of corn lying in the middle of the road.

It was probably some sort of tradition brought from the old country and passed down through the generations: just one of many strange things the Easters did. Us kids knew better than to ask questions about such doings; we just griped about them. (After Pa taught me the hickory switch dance, I griped silently.)

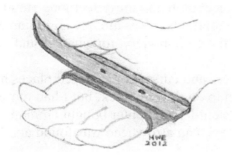

Corn shucker

On corn-shucking day, neighbors gathered in and shucked the owner's corn and stored it in his crib or granary. They solved all of the world's problems and some that hadn't yet happened. They talked about the good old days and found out who got caught doing what and who with. Everybody had "the best damn corn shucker God ever made." (A flat metal strip fastened to a piece of old shoe leather that fit on the hand (as seen above) that was used to help pull the shucks off the corn ears.)

They shucked the corn, threw the ears over the pile and threw the shucks behind. When everything got up to speed, the air was full of flying corn and tall tales. As the shuck piles grew higher, kids both young and old played in them.

On Grandpa's big day, Grandma cooked a huge corn-shucking dinner: with enough chicken and dumplings, pies, corn, green beans, cornfield peas, potatoes, cakes, biscuits, corn bread, lemonade, and skimmed milk to feed an army. Unlike at our house, she skimmed all the cream off the milk to make butter, which Grandpa sold at Kasco's Feed and Seed Store in Mt. Airy. That left the milk almost as good as water, but I drank it.

On occasion, a jar of moonshine was found down in the corn pile and it was a whole new deal: the granary got filled twice as fast and everybody went home happy. When another neighbor had a corn shucking, everybody gathered at his house and hoped for another jar of moonshine.

The very hardest jobs were done easier and faster when swapped with neighbors and when someone needed help, everybody gathered in. (Our log house, feed barn and tobacco barn were built with the help of neighbors.) When sickness, an accident or a death occurred, everybody brought in food, tended crops, cut firewood, cured tobacco and did what needed doing.

Other than meeting day at Crooked Oak Church and family re-unions, Grandpa and Grandma seldom got a break from the seven days a week routine of farming. For them, the plowing, hoeing, harvesting and feeding of the animals had to be done, "come Hell or high water."

Grandpa's everyday outfit was a pair of worn-out double-patched over-alls, the long-sleeved shirts he wore all summer, clodhopper shoes and an old floppy hat. He sweated fiercely and always looked about as tired and worn as his clothes. Grandma wore long sleeves, ankle-length dresses and a slatted cardboard bonnet made of cloth and neither of them got much of a tan.

Grandpa kept an eye on the sky and studied the clouds, the sundogs and the animals for signs of coming weather. He was always busy, but always took the time to answer my many questions. When Pa "took a little time off," Grandpa came by to check on us and when the big snows came, he cleared the road to our house with his home made horse-drawn snowplow.

While re-shoeing the horse one day, it slapped him with its tail. He slapped back with a rope and Grandma said, "Well, Pa, it was just after a horse fly." Grandpa said, "Who ever seen a horsefly this time of the year?"

While driving a fence post in the ground, he looked away, swung the axe and hit himself in the knee. Another day, he chopped his shoe with the axe and knew he was badly hurt, because he could feel blood running. He hurried home, pulled the shoe off, found no blood and the skin was barely marked.

When he first learned to talk, he would only speak the native tongue. He still remembered it and sometimes spoke Dutch to me. I had no idea what he was talking about, but one of the sayings was "Come around and have a seat in the corner." His everyday byword was, "Well, Sir" and when making plans for the future, he said, "If I live another year…"

One early Saturday morning, he hooked up his horse and wagon and headed for Mt. Airy to sell butter and eggs at Kasco's on Market Street. The twenty-five-mile round trip took all day and when he got back late in the day, (with a paper sack of candy for a certain person) both he and the horse were completely worn out. That was his last trip to town with the wagon and he began riding with Frank Coalson, who sold pickup loads of stove wood.

One day in Blackberry Summer, he and I hauled sacks of corn to Rossie Golding's Mill in his one-horse wagon. Rossie ground our corn into meal; I sold a bucket of blackberries at the store and spent all of the money for candy. It was almost like Christmas and our only wagon trip together. That was the day Grandpa became my hero.

George and Alice Easter   The George and Alice Easter home (1970s)
                                   (Courtesy of Ethel Calloway Smith and sons.)

The George Easter Home Place

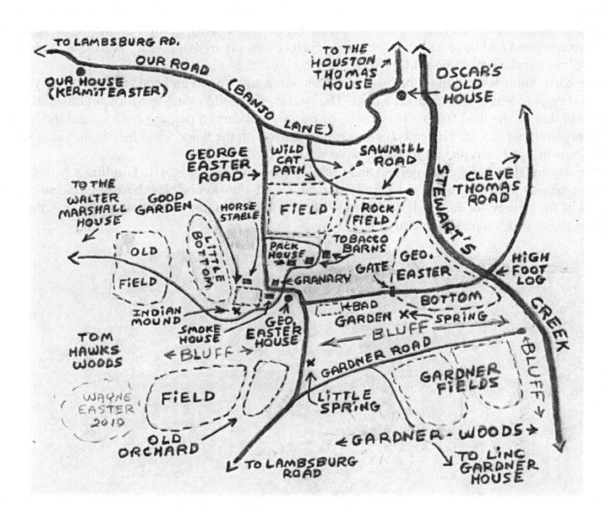

Chapter 9

The George Easter Home Place

The horse barn

The horse barn was about as old as the smoke house and stood beside the road to our house. It was made of logs, had a wood-shingle roof and two horse stalls divided by a tack room. The harness gear and saddle inside had been repaired many times with wire and twine, but it still worked.

When Grandma went on the warpath, Grandpa headed for his port in the storm: the tack room. He sat inside, whittled out new single trees and axe handles and hummed a folk song. In spring of the year, he cleaned out the stalls and hauled the manure away on his "slide" to fertilize the land and grow watermelons. Watermelons were what summer was all about and he grew them by the dozens in his patch on top of the hill.

A neighbor once invited kinfolks in for a Sunday watermelon feast and when they got there, he had no watermelons, because Grandpa had caught him red-handed trying to steal his. If he'd only asked, I'm sure Grandpa would've given him all he wanted. I sometimes "borrowed" one, but I was very careful to by-pass the big ones and I knew he didn't care.

When Grandpa died in 1947, Grandma gave me his saddle and the Lone Ranger headed west. While loping "Silver" down the pasture hill, the belly strap came loose and both saddle and myself wound up hanging upside down under the horse. The great western hero hung up his saddle that very day and headed back east. (When Mama sold our home place in 1985, my brother El found the saddle in the attic and called to see if I wanted to keep it. I now wish I had.)

The hog pen was just above the horse barn: also beside the road to our house. It was made of wire and planks and had a mud hole where the hog wallowed. The hotter the weather, the more it wallowed and the more it wallowed, the worse the mud hole stank. Grandpa and Grandma lived downwind and almost had to leave home in mid-summer.

The hog ate vegetable scraps from the kitchen mixed with water and hog food bought at Kasco's. It was said hogs would eat anything but cucumbers, but I never found out, because no hog ever got any of my cucumbers. All hogs ate well, because nobody wanted a skinny one at killing time. A fatter hog meant more lard, which was used for cooking all year and some became so fat they could no longer walk. They once ran free to eat chestnuts, which "fattened them up" and made the meat taste better. (I wondered how good old sausage could taste any better than it already did.) After blight killed all the chestnut trees in the 1920s, hogs no longer ran free.

Hog killing time came with the November frosts: another job we swapped with Grandpa. He shot his hog, hauled it to the scalding vat on the sled, rolled it into the hot water to scald it. Then he and Pa scraped the hair off with butcher knives, hung it up, cleaned it out, cleaned it up and chopped it up with an axe and a butcher knife.

No part of the hog was wasted, including the feet; tail and head, which became "souse meat." The hams, shoulders and side meat were "salted down" in the smoke house and Grandma ground sausage with a hand-cranked meat grinder, seasoned it, fried it, canned it and stored it in the basement. I figured all sausage was just " ordinary good old sausage," but Mama said Grandpa liked hers better than Grandma's. (I seriously doubt he ever mentioned that little fact to Grandma.)

The Grain'ry' (Grainary)

When Linc Gardner's first house burned, Grandpa bought his granary and re-assembled it across the road from the smoke house. He stored corn on the right side, (the downwind side) which had a slatted wall for air circulation. He stored animal feed in the left side, along with a corn sheller that made shelling corn easier than doing it by hand. (When Grandpa died, Grandma gave Pa the sheller.)

The two-stall cowshed was behind the granary: built of small logs with a plank roof and just like Jim Smith's, it was almost tall enough for the cow to get into. Old Bossy wore a bell that could be heard all day, unless she was far down the valley. If not back by milking time, they called her with a "swoooook, swoooook" sound and she came home to the cow gap. (A gap in the fence between two posts just wide enough for people to squeeze through.)

The cow was milked twice a day into a galvanized peck bucket: always from the cow's right side. "Don't you go doin' no milkin' from the left side, boy, or you'll be the one jumpin' over the moon." We brought a small amount of water in the bucket, just in case the cow's teats needed washing, which they often did. A scratch or cut on a teat was painful to the cow and she sometimes kicked the bucket and spilled the milk.

Even when not kicking, she constantly slapped with her tail, trying to outwit flies. She could snap it like a bullwhip and I was always in the line of fire. Just when I thought I could get on with the milking, she popped me in the eye again. (When Grandpa died, I stayed with Grandma that summer, milked her cow and squirted milk into her cat's mouths: the same cats I once chased from under the kitchen porch.)

A rusty barbed wire pasture fence ran from the cowshed, across the hill to the lower tobacco barn, turned right, led downhill and crossed the branch beside the ford. From the upper side of the shed, the fence ran uphill to a field, turned right and continued east almost to Stewart's Creek. Small tufts of hair from the cow's tail hung in some of the fence barbs.

Our pasture was never overloaded with grass, but the animals grazed on something all day. The very best grazing was about two feet outside the fence and when Pa saw Old Bossy pushing against the wire, he whacked her in the head with a hoe handle and gave her a piece of his mind. She didn't exactly die of fright and was soon attacking the fence again.

Grandpa tied a rope around his cow's neck one day and led her up the road toward the mailbox. They came back an hour later and he put her back in the pasture. Pa did the same with our cow and I wondered why anybody would take a cow for a stroll along the road.

It was a fact of life that the facts of life were not to be discussed at our house. Warren and I ran into many mysteries over the years, but with our terrific powers of deduction and logic, we finally solved the cow puzzle. It was amazing to learn that new calves didn't really come from a hollow log as we'd been told and we learned it long before old age set in.

The Pack House

A wagon road led from the smoke house uphill to Grandpa's pack house. It was made of logs, had a tin roof and a basement that smelled of tobacco all year. We stored cured tobacco inside in-season and off-season, we stored empty tobacco sticks, big burlap sacks and worn-out quilts.

A no-longer-used buggy sat under the side shelter. It had a faded black top, faded red wheels and had been parked for many years. As with most things, I learned the hard way that bumblebees built nests in the cracked black leather seat. The whole world was full of bee stingers and every single one had my name on it. When I even thought about a bee, wham, I got stung again.

Grandpa and Grandma once traveled in style, as they rode the buggy to town, church and family reunions. When Uncle Manuel got his first job, (in Galax) Pa hauled him to the top of Piper's Gap Mountain in the buggy. When it wore out, Grandpa and Grandma's only transportation was by horse, wagon and sled.

All one November day, we tied tobacco in the pack house basement, as rain fell on the tin roof. We were trying to get it all done before the market ended in December. Warren and I talked about all the bicycles, rifles, pocket watches and other great stuff we'd seen in the Sears Roebuck catalogue. Chances of getting much for Christmas were slim, but it didn't hurt to dream and we made sure certain people knew what we liked.

A Rusty Coat apple tree beside the pack house had apples the color of rusty iron, about as hard to bite, almost as good and nothing ate them except the hog. John Apples were a different story and Grandpa carried some in his coat pockets for snacks for himself, the horse and a starving grandson. Finding a worm in an apple was no big problem; I just whipped out my trusty Barlow, whittled it out and kept right on eating.

The two tobacco barns

The wagon road continued to Grandpa's two log tobacco barns on the hillside. A rusty fifty-gallon barrel sat under the drip-lines at each barn to catch the rainwater we used to make mud to seal the barn flues and fight fire if the flues got out of control. A plank in each barrel channeled more water from the eaves into the barrels. Mosquitoes laid eggs in the water that soon became "wiggle-tails" that soon became more mosquitoes that soon came searching for their favorite person in the whole world. They ate on me like they'd never had anything to eat before. Fact of the matter, I was probably their very first meal and I must've been good.

We cut flue wood in early spring, so it would be dry by curing time. We sawed the trees down, dragged them to the barn with the horse, sawed them into five-foot lengths and split them with a locust wedge and a hickory maul. Pa later bought a sledgehammer and a metal wedge that made the job easier. No matter how much flue wood we cut ahead of time, it was never enough and when the curing began, it vanished into thin air.

Each barn had two flues with two sets of heating pipes that snaked around inside and came back out on each side of the door. While curing, we kept an eye on the temperature with a thermometer that hung inside on a tier pole. When at it's hottest, it took almost no time to check it, get back outside and breathe again. We checked on the tobacco in the *top* of the barn by climbing a ladder around back. Hot, steamy air poured from the peephole and it took almost no time to check there either.

Grandpa's dilapidated lower barn in 1971

Grandpa's lower barn (seen above) had a shelter thatt furnished shade while twining tobacco and when curing all night, we parked the sleds under it to sleep in. They were snake and dew proof and I slept the night away covered up with old quilts, while Pa catnapped and kept the flue fires burning.

Tobacco sled

The tobacco sleds were ten feet long and four feet high, with Smith Douglas fertilizer sacks nailed on the inside to keep the tobacco from falling out. The horse pulled them through the fields and when full of tobacco leaves, they were dragged to the barn and traded for an empty one. When the runners wore out, Pa nailed white oak saplings on the bottoms and we kept on sledding.

Like most days, we rolled out of bed early on priming day, while the tobacco was still wet with morning dew. In almost no time, the primers were wet and cold, but as the sun and the temperature climbed, the dew dried up, the primers dried out and all too soon they were wet again: this time with sweat. The water jug ran dry often and needed refilling every time the sled driver hauled a load of tobacco to the barn. It was said some people never sweated and I wondered if they'd ever primed tobacco in a burning field in the middle of summer.

When priming the fields far from the barn, the barn workers got caught up between sled loads and took a break. When priming the closer fields, the primers stayed ahead and another sled-load was always waiting before the first one was twined. Having no rest periods made the day go faster.

Green tobacco had a sticky black gum that was almost impossible to wash off and when twining and priming, my hands got covered with it. That was exactly when certain places started itching: exactly those that couldn't be scratched in polite company. It was hard to stay calm when something was eating me alive and there was no place to hide and scratch. What a relief it was to sneak around behind the barn, back up against the wall and start rubbing.

The tobacco "twiner" my family used for many years. (2008)

Twining tobacco consisted of placing a tobacco stick in the notches on top of the twiner. (Seen above.) The "bunchers" handed small bunches of tobacco to the twiner person, who wrapped twine around them to hold them on the stick: a bunch on one side, then one on the other side until the sticks were full. The full sticks were then stacked on the ground and later hung on tier poles in the barn. The sticks were passed up to someone standing on the lower tier poles, then passed up to someone standing on the higher tier poles and the barn was filled from the top down.

When the tobacco had yellowed a few days, Pa fired the barn twenty-four hours a day at high temperature, When dried to a crisp, we left the barn door open so the tobacco would dampen enough to store in the pack house until selling time.

At selling time, we hung the cured tobacco in the basement to dampen again. We removed the leaves from the sticks, sorted them into different grades, tied them in "hands", bundled them into huge burlap bags and sold them at the auction warehouses in Mount Airy.

Our spring branch and another from the Fred Marshall house at Jim's Knob joined together and moseyed along beside Grandpa's Little Bottom. Another from the Tom Hawks Woods joined in near the Indian Mound. Grandpa's spring branch and the Little Spring branch joined in and everything meandered along through the pasture toward Stewart's Creek. All summer long, we played in the branch, chased minnows, caught crawfish and built rock and mud dams.

In hot dry weather, Grandpa parked his wagon in the branch ford and poured water on the wood parts of the wheels. That kept the metal rims from falling off when the wood parts became too dry. (In later years, Warren and I washed our cars there.)

Elderberries grew beside the branch ford; some became elderberry wine and others became elderberry jelly. The hollow stems became "popguns" and just like our slingshots, we were told, "Them things is dangerous, boys, they'll put your eyes out." Apparently, everything we did was dangerous to eyes, arms and legs and it was doubtful we'd ever live long enough to grow up.

Grandpa's pasture fence crossed the branch beside the ford and continued a hundred feet to a mile-long laurel bluff that began on Stewart's Creek and ended in the Tom Hawks Woods far up the valley. The fence turned left at the bluff, continued toward Stewart's Creek and was almost unneeded, because any cow or horse that could escape through the tangled mess deserved to be free.

The George Easter Road (Grandpa's Road) led from the ford and uphill through the bluff: the only break in the mile-long jungle. About halfway up the hill, the Little Spring came out from under some laurel bushes on the left. On hot summer days, tired travelers cooled in the shade, told tall tales and drank "the coldest water in the country." They talked about the good old days and did some of their best farming of the year, right there beside the spring.

Big sour blackberries grew across the road, except when a late freeze killed the blooms or they "blasted." As Sam Coalson told it, "If it rains the first three days in June, black berries'll "blast" and dry up and fall off the vine and never get ripe."

Grandpa's older worn-out orchard was on the hillside: with most of the trees dead or dying. Due to many years of farming between the rows and erosion, the apple and peach trees stood on ridges. Wild strawberries grew under the trees and bigger better tame ones grew in a strawberry patch on top of the hill. (That was one of the best things about Grandpa's place: good stuff to eat grew everywhere.)

The Gardner Road: on the left at the gate.) 2008

The Gardner Road branched left just above the Little Spring, leading to the two Gardner fields on Gardner's Ridge; just two of the many fields we sharecropped in the early years. At the first field, the road branched left, led by the second field and continued to Gardner's hickory trees beside Stewart's Creek. Even being so far from home, it was our favorite place to hunt squirrels.

Back at the first field, the Gardner Road forked right, led downhill by Gardner's spring and continued to the Linc Gardner home place over the next hill. After Linc died in 1935, nobody lived there for several years and his huge Gardner Woods were one of my favorite places to ramble. Back on the George Easter Road, (Later named Watershed Road) it continued by another of Grandpa's upland fields, through the Gardner Woods and on to our mailboxes on Lambsburg Road.

We got very little mail in the early years and with the box so far from home, we seldom checked by. That changed when I ordered a super duper special edition pocket watch just like the railroad used, with satisfaction guaranteed, or double your money back. I tried to meet the mailman every day until it came and when it finally did, he (Mont Worrell) was as pleased as me.

Back at the branch ford, the Cleve Thomas Road led east through the pasture toward Stewart's Creek. A row of no-longer-used telephone poles stood on the left side and Grandpa's worn-out "bad" garden was across the road on the right. It was fenced with barbed wire, which was almost wasted, because nothing grew well there. Just beyond was a half-acre of ivy (mountain laurel) bushes: with brown spots on the leaves. Since the Woodruff Company only bought ivy with perfectly green leaves, we broke no ivy there.

A moss-covered tree that had fallen across the branch became my bridge into the bluff. Pa told me, "Nobody with no sense don't go climbing in them bluffs, boy. They's things in there that'll eat you alive." (During all my rambles in the bluff, I never saw any of them.) A "one-berry" bush grew on the fallen log, with one bright red berry in the top. It looked good enough to eat, but I'd been warned, "They's stuff out yonder that'll put your lights out and anything you don't know nothing about, you better leave it alone." (Apparently, the world was full of calamities and disasters and every one of them was just waiting to wipe me out.)

Bluff Climbing was dirty work and Mama sometimes threatened to disown me. Best I could tell, my storybook heroes in the Great North Woods never got dirty, never had to take a bath and if they had a Mama giving orders, I never read about it. Why me, oh Lord?

Some gallon-sized rocks had "accidentally" rolled down through the pasture from the rocky hilltop cornfield and landed in the Cleve Thomas Road. Fact of the matter, Warren and I were testing the theory of gravity and sure enough, every single one of them rolled downhill. Other than my family, very few people used the road, so nobody got hurt.

Our son Mike where the drawbar gate once stood at Grandpa's Bottom (1971)

The Cleve Thomas Road continued through a drawbar pasture gate and through the middle of Grandpa's Bottom. It crossed the ford at the High Foot Log on Stewart's Creek and continued to Cleve Thomas's house over the hill. When we sharecropped Dave Carson's two small bottoms farther downstream, we hauled wagonloads of corn back across the ford in fall of the year.

The High Foot Log was first-class, as foot log go; it hung high in the air, had a handrail to hang onto and planks nailed on it to walk on: a great place to sit and daydream on hot summer days and watch fish swim by.

The bottom was Grandpa's best land, where he grew corn there every year. Occasional floods brought in new dirt to renew the land and it never wore out. Compared to upland fields, soft bottomlands were a paradise to hoe corn in: if there was any such thing.

A million water-worn creek rocks grew in a small upper area of the bottom and more came up after every rain. A huge pile beside the road became bigger every year, as more were added to it. "You boys stay offa' that rock pile, 'cause they's copperheads in there as mean as snakes and they don't like nobody." I sat on the rock pile and watched Grandpa harvest oats with a cradle. His long-sleeved shirt and overalls were drowned with sweat as he cut and stacked the oats into sheaves that looked like those in Blum's Almanac.

Back up the valley at Grandpa's house, a "slide-road" led from the smoke house, passed by the Good Garden and the Indian Mound and climbed straight uphill to another worn-out field. To get the plow uphill to the field, Pa wedged a three-foot pole in the frame and when the horse pulled the plow, it was lifted off the ground. He and the horse then scrambled and clawed as they climbed the hill in a cloud of dust, with the plow riding on the pole. Pa fought to hang onto the plow handles and I wouldn't have been surprised if he, the plow and the horse had taken flight into the air.

Some worn-out apple and peach trees grew in one end of the worn-out field and we only grew corn there one year. Like all old fields, it eventually grew up in broom straw, blackberry vines and sassafras bushes. The road continued through the woods to Walter Marshall's house at the Big Curve on Lambsburg Road.

The Little Bottom (March 2002)

Corn grew best in bottoms, as well as certain pests, whose sole aim in life was to bite, sting and gnaw on me. Fodder worms were mean, green, almost square little creatures about an inch long that ate on the corn blades (leaves) and they knew how to sting. They were plentiful in late summer: especially in the Little Bottom just west of the horse barn. Pulling fodder required little attention to the job and I was usually daydreaming about other things in other places. The first sting instantly brought me back to the cornfield and nobody had to tell me to pay attention.

Chinquapins grew on a hillside at the south-end and I could hardly wait for them to ripen in September. Sassafras bushes also grew there, but no trees were allowed to grow tall and shade the bottom. Just like the chestnut trees, all of the chinquapin bushes eventually died.

Leaving Grandpa's house in any direction meant going uphill, except toward Stewart's Creek. Instead of sensibly going around the hill by the tobacco barns as it once had, the road to our house (Grandpa's Road) went straight up a steep hill. It was a hard climb for people, horses, wagons and automobiles and nobody could "pull it" on a bicycle. Going downhill was a great ride but going back up was a long hard push. With very little automobile traffic, nobody worried about keeping it repaired and it stayed washed-away by gully-washer-storms.

About halfway up the hill was an old sawmill place on the right side of the road, one of at least a dozen in our area. More chinquapins and huckleberries grew in a sprout patch across of the road. Both grew well where all the trees had been cut, but like the chinquapins at the Little Bottom, they too eventually died.

Grandpa's Road continued by his best up-land field on the hill top, where he grew corn, tobacco and watermelons every year: where he caught a neighbor stealing his watermelons and where I set my short-lived bobwhite trap.

Beyond the field, the road continued along the ridge and joined our road. (Later named Banjo Lane.) Turning right on our road led to Oscar Marshall's Old House on Stewart's Creek and turning left led by our house and on to the Lambsburg Road a half-mile away at the foot of Jim's Knob.

From the left: Pa, Aunt Maude, Grandpa, and Grandma in the 1920s

Grandpa died alone on Stewart's Creek one dark snowy day in March 1947. Pa was spring-plowing our tobacco field, when Harry Smith came running up the road on his mule and told us Grandpa had died. It was the most impossible thing I'd ever heard.

Grandpa had gone hunting on Stewart's Creek and when he failed to come home at dinnertime, Grandma went down the Cleve Thomas Road to check on him. He was already gone when she found him lying beside the High Foot Log: with his arm under his head for a pillow like I'd seen him do when taking a nap in the floor.

We never knew what happened, but he'd been in the creek and his clothes were wet. Neighborhood men gathered around on the creek bank and tried to figure it out. Big snow flakes kept falling and somebody said, "Snow don't amount to much this time of the year."

I've always hoped Grandpa died doing the stuff he liked: being outdoors, prowling the creek banks in all kinds of weather, keeping an eye on the sky for a weather forecast and searching for signs of a new season. Whatever happened, Stewart's Creek was never again like it was before and we both lost a great friend.

I'd always considered Grandpa's place to be my own and some of my best memories are of him, his farm and his patience. He was always busy, but never too busy to answer my many questions. He knew all the important things: like when snow was coming, how bad the winter would be, when fish would bite best and best of all, he figured if tomorrow came, it would be a another good day. What else did anybody need to know?

I stayed with Grandma at night that summer and slept in the feather bed. One morning in the wee hours, one of her cats woke me up meowing and hanging on the window screen. I could tell it was scared to death, but it had nothing on me. Even though I was Grandma's brave protector, no way was I about to go out there to find out what the problem was.

Grandma sold the farm that fall and lived with my Aunt Maude until she died: November 20, 1963.

A flyer advertising the sale of the George Easter Farm
(Courtesy of Curtis Easter.)

No year is shown in the above flyer, but according to a perpetual calendar, the above month and day are correct for 1947.

Watershed Lake, seen from the George Easter home place (2002)

Part 4

Hunter, fisherman, scout, scholar…

Graduation class at Beulah School (1950)

From the left: James Lawson, Wayne Easter, J W York, Runell Lowe, Cicero Gregory, Bessie McCormick, Tommy Creed, Ina Mae Bryant, Ed Clifton, Carrie Smith, Willie Collins, Ina Smith and Bill Lundy.

Chapter 10

School

The new Beulah School (Late 1940s)

Our southern sky glowed bright orange the night the old Beulah School burned in the 1930s and a new one opened in 1937. It was my first day of school, Mama helped me up into the bus and told the driver, (N A "Bill " Lowe) "Take care of my little boy.

The bus route ended at Walter Marshall's house on Lambsburg Road and we warmed by his fireplace until bus time. The route later ended at the foot of Mailbox Hill, where several mailboxes marked the end of the mail route; it was a longer walk and we no longer stayed warm. A shelter made of sawmill slabs kept us out of the weather, but with games to play and races to run, who worried about such stuff? In later years, both the bus and mail routes were extended to the Virginia state line, which was closer to home.

The bus ran the twenty-mile round trip to school each weekday, except when it snowed. Highway 89 was the only paved road and all others became a muddy mess in winter. The worst place was a low swag on Pine Ridge Road beyond Lovill's Peach Orchard and when at its worst, nobody could drive through it. When the bus got stuck, we just sat there and pouted and starved until somebody pulled us out.

I saw great wonders that first day of school: one being a chimney so tall you had to "fall over backwards" to see that high. It was as tall as the clouds and had its own black cloud of coal smoke boiling out of the top. Another sight was a huge windmill on a tall steel tower that pumped water for the whole school.

Nobody did anything like we did it back on Stewart's Creek: nobody sawed wood with a crosscut saw, nobody started fires with kerosene oil, or carried water from a spring. They just turned a little wheel on a radiator thing and the rooms got warm and pushing a button on a thing-a-ma-jig brought more water than an army could drink. Another big wonder was indoor bathrooms, when we didn't even have an outhouse.

My older cousin Harry Smith helped me get inside the building and find my room. There was big auditorium surrounded by classrooms and more people than I'd ever seen before. Somehow, I made it through the first day, didn't get lost, got on the right bus and made it back home to Mama, all in one piece.

Lunch, recess and art classes were the best parts of school and I spent many happy hours drawing pictures of airplanes, cars and houses. What I liked least was all that time we wasted trying to add a bunch of dumb numbers. When recess finally came, the older kids played baseball in the red-dirt ball field and the younger kids played hide and seek, tag, marbles, mumble-de-peg and chased each other on the big cement cover of the school's septic tank.

Having almost no money, I brought lunch from home in a lard bucket. On rare occasions, the Gods smiled and Mama sent a half-gallon fruit jar of home-canned green beans to pay for my lunch for a week. We had no electricity at home and the small glass bottles of ice-cold milk in the lunchroom were out of this world.

Skull Camp Mountain from Highway 89 near Beulah School

I could see Skull Camp Mountain out the schoolhouse window and tried to keep an eye on it and the teacher at the same time. Old timers told hair-raising tales about the mountain and just like No Man's Land; the very name caused chill bumps. I daydreamed of climbing all the way to the top, where somebody found a skull at a campsite a long time ago.

When the leaves changed color in October, I could see hickory trees on the mountain, because they were the darkest yellow of all. "*That* was what they should be teaching in school: important things like how to find hickory trees for squirrel hunting, how to be a scout and hunter and how to survive in the wilderness."

Airplanes, fishing, hunting and building forts were high priorities in my world, along with pocketknives, slingshots, windmills and things that flew. "Who had time for all that 'rithmetic stuff nobody would ever use?

During the Big War, I whittled out my own airplane from scrap lumber and even though it never got off the ground, untold German and Japanese fighter planes went down in flames. I whittled out wooden windmills that worked great if I ran fast enough. By applying my vast whittling knowledge and watching school pals who were smarter than me, I learned how to make them spin at high speed. Thomas Edison would never know it, but heavy competition was coming down the Pike.

When I was just about to go down in history, a teacher with a big paddle (Virgie Lowe) got on our bus, called me up-front and whaled the devil out of me right there in front of the whole world. (She had already warned me about running windmills out the bus window.) I told her I didn't have my hand out very far, but she still "laid it on me." It didn't hurt too bad, but it took all of the wind out of my sails. Since I could no longer use the bus window, my high-speed aeronautics experiments came to an abrupt end and Thomas Edison once again rested in peace.

Just like back on Stewart's Creek, danger lurked everywhere in the schoolhouse. A set of ladder-type steps behind the auditorium stage led up to a window on the schoolhouse roof. They were very high, very hard to climb and very off limits to school kids. A certain red-blooded scout knew a challenge when he heard one and first chance he got, he headed for the roof.

While climbing alone near the top one fateful day, I slipped and fell. The stage floor was "way down yonder" and if not for a ceiling beam three feet below, I would've been the late Mr. Easter. My only wound was a bruised sensitive area in the straddle where the beam caught me. I never told anybody about my last attempt to play on the schoolhouse roof and when people asked why I was walking funny, I just kept limping along.

I'd just written something on the blackboard, when it and the frame fell and whacked me on the head. I already knew some of the stars and constellations, but when the blackboard fell out of the sky, I got a crash course in astronomy. Bells rang, lights flashed and Mars, Venus, Pluto and Saturn circled all around my head right in front of everybody, right there in the classroom; right there in broad day light. (My first thought was that the teacher was trying to pound some knowledge in my head.)

While dozing in class another day, another teacher said, "If Wayne don't start doing his homework, I'm going to get him." I'd never heard of homework, but when she explained how it all worked, I was the best homeworker she ever had. The last thing I needed was to get "got" right in front of the whole class. Still another teacher told the class to stand up. Then she looked at me and said, "You stand up too, Wayne." I told her, "I *am* standing up." She almost had to dismiss class to stop the hee-hawing.

One warm spring day, we marched single-file along Highway 89 to Minnie's/Millie's Spring at the foot of Skull Camp Mountain. I'd never been on a picnic before and it was all we'd talked about for days. The way I looked at it, anything was better than being in a dumb class room all day "doin' 'rithmatic."

We played games and chased each other for hours on what was one of the best school days I'd ever seen. Just before I died of starvation, we built a fire, roasted hot dogs and marshmallows and drank the R C Colas we had cooling in the spring. Right then and there, picnics went straight to the top of my "best things to do" list.

I was moping along in reading class one day, when some words in a book about some talking chickens got my attention. Even I knew our chickens back home had never talked, at least not to me, but some of the words began making sense. What a strange feeling it was to learn that words in a book could draw pictures in my mind.

The world changed forever and reading became as important as recess, picnics and girls. I read about the Great North Woods, the Wild West; pirates and buried treasure and was never again without a book to read.

Most families in the Beulah School area were farmers and it was a given that sons would become farmers like their dads. Terry Beamer taught the FFA class (Future Farmers of America) and we learned many up-to-date things about farming, none of which we did back home.

The way we did everything on Stewart's Creek was sealed in concrete and this educated son knew better than to go home and tell Pa how to farm. On top of that, there was no way to show him how to use modern machinery when we didn't have any.

Trying to improve on perfection was out of the question, because everything we did was done in the right moon sign and in the right order, which we'd refined down to a science. When a field completely wore out, we did as Grandpa and his Grandpa had done before him; we cleared off another new ground and continued right along, just like God intended.

I didn't really care how many more bushels of corn per acre we could grow by practicing soil conservation; we'd already hauled so many wagonloads out of Oscar Marshall's creek bottoms, I never wanted to see another ear of corn. There were more important things to do, like fishing, hunting, prowling Stewart's Creek and exploring No Man's Land.

The school smoking ground was located at a small cemetery beside the schoolhouse. Most people "rolled their own" with Golden Grain, Prince Albert, or homegrown tobacco, but those with money smoked "ready-mades." When everybody got fired up, it looked like the cemetery was on fire. I started smoking about 1949, when it became the grown-up thing to do. (As it came to be, quitting was a lot harder than starting.)

During the Big War, Beulah School held a scrap-metal drive and us school kids brought stuff from home on the school bus. We didn't have much of anything lying around home, metal or otherwise, but I brought pieces of a junked car and some worn-out plow points. We also saved tinfoil from cigarette packages and chewing gum wrappers. The pile of scrap metal soon became as big as a house and from all the praise the teachers laid on us; I figured Beulah School won the war all by itself.

As time went by, I ran out of fingers and toes and was forced to learn to count. With some tender loving care and tremendous patience, some dedicated teachers taught me to add, subtract, work fractions and do other unnecessary evils.

Two of the best were Mrs. Allen, who was slightly crippled and Mr. Cooper, who talked about the important things in life: the future, the planets and outer space. (At least, one other Earthling knew how the world turned.) As happened, the teacher I liked least (Mrs. Council) taught me the most and somehow, I made it through twelve years without a single teacher going insane.

Our senior class graduated in 1950 and it became my job to predict our future. I built a time machine (a wooden box with knobs and an antenna) in the school woodworking shop to help me decide where we were headed. Best I could tell, great things were coming down the pike for thirteen lucky people. We could just kick back and relax, because each of us would become famous and a certain kid from Stewart's Creek would become the *most* famous.

From the auditorium stage on graduation night, I fired up my amazing invention and introduced the audience to the world's future leaders. I assured them they were looking at tomorrow's explorers, astronomers, rocket scientists, and millionaires and Beulah School had "done good."

Apparently, the future didn't think like me, because my famous machine turned out to be no more accurate than its maker, who'd never completely understood Blum's Almanac. As happened, not a single one of my predictions came true.

I graduated on top of the world and at the bottom of the class, with no idea of what to do next. I picked green beans at an over-the-mountain farm for a week, but figured that was no career, because green beans only grew in summer and I didn't even like the cussed things to eat.

I then picked peaches at Lovill's Peach Orchard on Pine Ridge Road for a few days: figuring to live on peaches the rest of the summer and make a fortune at the same time. After the first bellyfull, I didn't even like peaches anymore and on top of that; the orchard was hotter than a July tobacco field. Even worse was the itchy peach fuzz that got into places I didn't even know existed After a couple of weeks of itching, scratching misery, my peach-picking career came to an end and I headed back to Pa's tobacco fields.

Before graduation, our class had filled out forms with the State Employment Security Commission and soon after the peach-picking disaster; a letter came suggesting an interview at Carolina Industrial Plastics Company in Mt. Airy. With all my 12 years of schooling, I'd known all along, it was just a matter of time. With such an important sounding name, no way could it be anything but a great place to work. I could already see myself in a white shop coat, with a pencil behind my ear, carrying a clipboard in a laboratory-type environment and solving all the world's problems. The world had finally beaten a path to my door and I'd soon be living on Easy Street. (It didn't exactly work out that way.)

I was interviewed by a Mr. Lewis Webb, who said I was a little on the short side, but they'd get me a pop crate to stand on. Instead of a laboratory, they put me in a huge building full of machines running wide-open and making so much noise I couldn't hear what anybody said. If I'd had a car, I'd have gone back home to Mama that very day. (Since I'd already walked the dozen miles in the wee hours one Saturday night, no way would that happen again.)

Somehow I got through the first day and the next was easier. In spite of all my schooling, there were a few minor things to learn. In fact, to keep the job, I had to learn quite a few things. The tools were more complicated than Pa's plow wrenches, auger and handsaw and even more complicated than Jim Smith's monkey wrench.

As it came to be, the job required knowing some of the very stuff I'd learned at Beulah School that I'd never need: such as arithmetic and fractions. Somehow, I got through the first few days without getting fired or shot and learned to do it like they wanted it done.

My machine at the "Plastic Plant" (1950s)

For the next two and a half years, the "Plastic Plant" was my second home, during which I bought two cars, totaled both and lost my driver's license for a year for DUI. Soon after, (in spring of 1953) a letter came from the draft board saying I'd been selected by my neighbors to serve my country in times of need.

The Korean War was raging full blast and having already won WW2 with a pile of scrap metal, I figured I might as well win another one. Unfortunately, the powers-that-be heard I was coming and stopped the fighting while I was still in basic training. (I think what happened was, the North Koreans heard General Easter was coming and threw down their guns and ran.)

Unlike back at Beulah School, the army lost no time in telling me whose butt was in trouble if I didn't pay attention. They didn't care how well I hunted squirrels on Jim's Knob, or how well Mama shot the shotgun; I would shoot the rifle and do everything their way, which was by the numbers, or else. The words "or else" got my attention and nobody listened better than me.

Thanks to the patient help of my teachers back at Beulah School, I'd already learned how to learn and without them, I would've either been on permanent k p or in the stockade. After drowning the sand-hills of Fort Jackson with my sweat and blood, I made it through basic training with the best tan ever and a small beginning of self-confidence.

Fighting the war in Myrtle Beach 1953   Fighting the war in Germany 1954

After a few weeks of wheeled-vehicle maintenance school at Fort Jackson, my best pal and I made a hundred on the final test. It was my first ever and my teachers back at dear old Beulah High would've been proud. We won a weekend pass to Myrtle Beach: including free food and lodging at Myrtle Beach Air Force Base. We ate too much, drank too much and kept a close eye on the pretty girls as they paraded along the beach.

After a few more weeks of tracked-vehicle maintenance school at Fort Knox, I became a mechanic and could fix tanks, trucks, jeeps and other stuff, sometimes. I was stationed in Fort Lewis and later volunteered to go to Germany. With Russia "just over the hill," we trained constantly, slept in the snow and kept an eye on "them Rooskies." Once again, I think my reputation had preceded me and they were afraid to start anything. Except for some beer joint brawls, where I wound up with a crooked nose, I did no actual fighting and made it back home o k.

I was discharged in April of 1955, returned to the Plastic Plant and was immediately sent to school to train on new machines. (Apparently, I'd be going to school the rest of my life.) After spending a fortune ($5.00) to have my car radio repaired, I found my calling: just go to school a few days, (just what I needed) learn how to plug tubes into radios and the big money would come rolling in. Then I could live on Easy Street the rest of my days. (Once again, it didn't quite work out like that.)

I attended two years of night school under the G I Bill (while still working at the Plastic Plant) and after some early-on failures, learned how to repair my car radio. For the next fifty years, I worked for other companies and owned my own business twice, as a seller and fixer of home electronics. In the meantime, the schools and learning continued and to this day, I have yet to learn it all and the big money has yet to come rolling in, but it'll probably happen any day now.

Chapter 11

Winter Crop

Makin' likker'

    The Great Depression bought no great changes in how we lived; we just kept doing as we'd always done, we "growed" our own food, made our own likker' and walked everywhere we went. As Pa said it, "Buyin' stuff at the store takes money, boys and we ain't got none,"
    We planted every cornfield he could find, because corn was how we lived. With a barn full of fodder and tops and a granary full of corn, everybody and everything had food for winter. Some of our corn became corn meal, most of which became corn bread. On occasion, some of it became moonshine far back into the hills. No way could we have survived without corn.
    Making moonshine was "agin' the law," which was like waving a red flag in front of a bull for true mountain people, "If the Givermint' can make likker' I can too and mine's a whole lot better and a whole lot cheaper." Those who made moonshine knew their woods far better than the "revenoors" and seldom did anyone get caught.
    Anyone who breathed air was an expert at making, buying, selling, testing, drinking and talking about moonshine. If it was made right, it was crystal clear and held a "good solid bead" when the jar was shook. Pa's "Winter Crop" as he called it, passed every test known to mankind and was so good; he couldn't decide whether to sell it or drink it.
    On occasion, he sold some "sellin likker" to keep us out of the Dobson Poor House. Never lived the thirsty buyer who could resist his sales-pitch, "This is the best stuff I ever made." (It was great to know it was made right in our own back yard by my very own Pa.)
    Making moonshine was hard work, but when the owner wrapped himself around some of his best, it was "Katy, bar the door." After "downing a few good shots," he could climb every mountain and outrun any lawman ever made. Word was that an automobile became a rocket when some moonshine was poured into its gas tank. I never saw it done, because few people in our world had a gas tank to pour it in and nobody was about to waste good likker.'
    I had no idea what a lawman looked like, but after eavesdropping on my parents, I figured it out: they were big, bad, ugly, had horns and worst of all, they were out there and sneaked up on still places when nobody was looking and put people out of business in nothing flat. On top of that, they gave the still owner a free vacation in someplace called Atlanta and taught him the joys of making little rocks out of big rocks.

When running a still, the operator had a definite need-to-know when the law was coming and washtubs got beaten, rocks appeared on fence posts, bed sheets appeared in trees, dogs were turned loose and shotguns boomed. A shotgun blast was unreliable, because the still operator had no way of knowing if it was a warning or a rabbit hunter, which cause some unnecessary running. (One big requirement for running a still was being a fast runner, because at any moment, you could be running for your life.) The best warning of all was the dog, which was supposed to be tied up back home. When his own dog showed up at the still place, he knew it was long past time to head for the hills.

When making moonshine, Pa kept his ear to the ground and Old Betsy leaning against a handy tree: ready to shoot, head for tall timber or both "You can't do nothin' without a shotgun." Thanks to the powers that be, the law population didn't decrease any on his account and he never had to shoot anybody or shoot *at* anybody.

Laurel thicket

The best place to set up a still was beside a spring branch deep in the backwoods under a laurel thicket. Pa liked to set up where the law had just searched and even then, he didn't stay in one place very long. Even while his still was cooking, he was thinking about where to set up next.

Making moonshine was not for the weak and meek, because everything had to be toted in by manpower: the still, worm, thumper barrel, water bucket, cornmeal, sugar and fruit jars, as well as planks to make mash boxes and dry firewood, which made less smoke. "You see smoke coming outta' one a' them hollers' boy, keep your-you-know-what outa'a there or you'll get it shot off."

Pa's basic recipe was a close-guarded secret, but corn meal and sugar were the two main ingredients. He mixed up a new batch in the mash boxes and covered them with planks to keep 'possums, coons and other "ungodly varmints" from drowning inside. When the conglomeration had fermented for a length of time determined by the seasons, the phase of the moon, daily temperatures and the secret ingredients, Pa was ready to "haul the mail," as he said it.

He built a fire under the still, filled it with mash and placed the cap on top, with a heavy rock to hold it down when the pressure rose. As the mash heated, pressure forced the steam through the still cap, into a thumper barrel and through a condenser pipe cooled with branch water.

As the steam cooled, it condensed into moonshine and came out of the condenser pipe into a bucket. Pa then strained it through an old felt hat to get the bugs and trash out, added water for tempering and poured it into fruit jars.

Every batch he made was better than the last one and as he said it, "This here stuff's too good to sell, boy. We gonna' mash back and sell the next run. They's drinkin' likker and they's selling likker and I ain't sellin' none this good."

The bluff at Oscar's Big Bottom (1971)

It was Pa's God-given right to make moonshine on his or anybody else's land, especially if they didn't know about it. I once helped him set up beside a small spring branch in the bluff above Oscar Marshall's Big Bottom on Stewart's Creek. (Seen above.) Armed with slingshot and a pocket full of rocks, I stood watch under a shade tree on top of the hill. I had no idea what a lawman looked like, but I was supposed to holler and run if I saw one. Thank my lucky stars I never saw one.

Insurance

We hid the full fruit jars far away in other woods, as insurance against hard times. There must have been an epidemic of hard times in years gone by, because I found old still places along almost all backwoods streams. Pa was a lucky man and his only still accident happened when a pressure cap blew off the still and his face got burned; he wouldn't tell me why he quit shaving.

On occasion, he sold some of his "best stuff" to some rough looking people who came by our house; the kind you'd never want to meet on a dark road at midnight. He told them, "Light and come in" and when they did, I stayed ready to head for the hills, in case trouble broke out. As ugly as they were, I could tell they were glad to see Pa and he was glad to see them and I never had to run.

As tradition demanded, the buyers shook the jar to see if beads formed around the top, then made the most important test, the taste test. To a man, the buyers told Pa, "That's the best stuff I ever seen." That was good to hear, because it meant money coming in, which we always needed, always. They sampled a while, jawed a while, sampled some more, everybody's outlook improved and they all went home happy.

Pa kept his "private stash" hidden behind a log in Oscar Marshall's Woods and when the path to it became too worn, he hid it in a hole in a hollow black gum tree: the same place I hid secret war maps and other important documents. He stored his at the bottom and I stored mine up in the tree.

In later years, he hid it in the granary, which didn't require a long walk in the woods. When his best pals came by, they were given a free tour inside to check out the cured ham and fatback and the long-range weather forecasts. Sometimes that took a while.

Somewhere in the woods and fields was a cure for every known ailment; you just had to know what it was and where to find it. The list of remedies varied from boiled pine needles, burning pine knots and pine rosin, to willow bark, sassafras tea and ginger root. Throw in some store-bought stuff like Black Draught, Rosebud Salve and Vick's Vaporub and no sickness dared come within five miles. Top off any of the above with a few good shots of moonshine and you'd probably live forever.

Some grown-ups were sick quite often and were never without their "snakebite medicine." Even when snow was a foot deep, they kept an eye out for copperheads, "cause you can't never tell when one'll come crawlin' back outta' the ground."

"Good" moonshine was the best medicine known and cured a "whole passel" of ills: like warts, mange, distemper, flu, snakebites, bad colds, old age and bad news. At one house, a fruit jar full sat on the kitchen table at all times: guaranteed to do everything but wake the dead. Drink enough of it, and even if it didn't cure your problem, you felt so good it no longer mattered. (Next morning, you had whole new set of problems and felt "worser than ever.")

We had our own special cure for colds, flu and the croup; we poured a small amount of moonshine in a saucer, lit it with a match and it burned with a blue flame. We blew the flame out, then drank it and no doubt about it, the magic blue flame cured the problem.

My favorite medicine of all time was a mixture of vinegar, sugar and baking soda that made a fizz bomb. It made you belch, sneeze, wheeze and it kept fizzing in your nose even after you drank it. It was guaranteed to ambush a cold at the pass.

Warren and I were forced (under treat of bodily harm with a hickory switch) to take Black Draught, whether we were sick or not and it was the worst tasting stuff on Earth. Anything that could make you sick was afraid to come near it. As bad as the burned likker' tasted, Black Draught was worse by a mile.

Pa told of two men who had too much to drink the night before, "Sanford was in terrible bad shape next morning and flat out of anything to drink. His buddy Sam went to a certain house to get Sanford some "hair of the dog" to save his life, Sure enough, a certain feller' at a certain house just happened to have the right stuff. Sam figured to sample it to see if it was up to par and took a great big swig. He smacked his lips and said, "I think Sanford's gittin' better already." (I've always wondered if poor old Sanford survived.)

Pa and my Uncle Claude were sitting at the kitchen table one night, sampling some of Pa's latest run. Uncle Claude sang a song and played his imaginary banjo, with the song going something like, "Eleven cent cotton and forty cent meat, how in the world can a poor man eat?" The banjo sounds went something like, "Ponkalaka, ponkalaka, ponkalaka, pow." At the word "pow," he slammed his fist down on the table and broke our oil lamp chimney. I jumped a foot off the floor and cried, because I figured we'd be in the dark forever.

One memorable day, Pa and I fired up the A-Model and headed for Scraptown to buy some moonshine. I was a little leery, because Scraptown's reputation was enough to scare the socks off a dead man. Word was that the word Scrap had nothing to do with junk and people who lived there liked nothing better than a little face-to-face with baseball bats or whatever was handy.

I sweated all the way there and we finally stopped at a shack up on the side of the mountain. A big ugly man with a big ugly rifle came out, along with a pack of foxhounds that were about to eat the doors off the car. I looked all around for a place to run, just in case. He glared at us and asked what we were doing in "these parts."

When Pa told him why we were there, they became friends, sampled a while and told tall tales. Pa finally bought a whole case of moonshine, we headed for home and I breathed again. We took the long way back and as we chic-a-lacked along the back roads, the radiator started boiling and Pa got "all uptight", just like I'd been all along. No way did we need car trouble right in the middle of "all them mean Scrap Towners." Worst of all, what if the law came along? With us having a load of moonshine on board, no way could we outrun anybody, especially with an A-Model.

We sweated along, built up a huge head of steam and just when the car was ready to blow up, we came to a branch that ran across the road. We re-filled the radiator with a tin can, kept an eye out for trouble and finally got under way again. Pa breathed a big sigh of relief, I breathed again and thanks to his expert driving and pure blind luck, we made it back home without getting caught, shot or having to fight anybody.

I'd just bought my first car, when a neighbor thumbed a ride home with me from Mount Airy. He had me stop at a house on Highway 89 near Fred Jarrell's General Store. We walked uphill to the house, he bought a pint of moonshine and put it in an inside coat pocket. When we got back to the car, Sheriff Sam Patterson was standing beside it.

He asked my cohort in crime, "Simon, What you got in that coat pocket?" When Simon opened up his coat, showed the sheriff the pint bottle and said, "Nothing," I could already see jail bars in my immediate future. Sheriff Sam said, "That's a mighty suspicious house you just came out of, so you better be careful." (I was very, very careful as we drove away.)

One warm Saturday afternoon, my "grown-up" pals and I stocked up on beer at Carl Nunn's beer joint on Highway 89, then headed for the parking lot at Chestnut Grove Church in Lambsburg. Our big plans were to make music in the shade of the oak trees, sip some suds, watch the pretty girls walk by and keep an eye on Sugar Loaf Mountain.

I was driving, somehow lost control and slid out of the road into a gatepost. As we checked out the broken post, a couple of cars came by, but nobody stopped. Just after we got under way again, we met a Virginia Trooper, who stopped us and asked if we'd seen a wreck back over the road. Of course we hadn't "seen no wreck" and went on our merry way.

We canceled our big plans, I took my buddies home and wasted no time getting out of Virginia. When I got back home, the Trooper was waiting for me and Pa had to go with us to Hillsville to keep me out of jail. I learned right away that lawmen were smarter than I'd thought and ever after, when I met a Virginia trooper, I prayed he could see the big halo hanging over my head.

Moonshine can be hard to find on today's Stewart's Creek and a dry spell has been known to happen. Thanks to a few old timers who cling to the old ways, the dry spells are temporary and some of "the best stuff ever made" can still be found on certain back roads. You just need to speak the Stewart's Creek lingo, have some grits in your voice, some green stuff hanging out of your pocket and tell 'em Joe sent you. You can't miss.

Work

Play

Chapter 12

Work and Play

No matter what was happening down on Stewart's Creek, work came first at our house. We fed the animals, gathered eggs, "got in" wood, carried water from the spring, milked the cow morning and night and cooled the milk in the spring box. At meal times, up to the house it went and if any was left over, back down the hill it went again. Next day, we did it all over again.

We split pine knots to start started fires in the heater and cook stove. They were slower than kerosene, but only cost a little time and effort and were everywhere on the backside of Jim's Knob: the remains of pine trees killed by a wild fire in the 1930s.

Everything we did burned wood and keeping enough for the heater and cook stove was a full-time job. We were told in no uncertain terms, "You boys get some stove wood in here tonight so I can start a fire in the mornin', or they won't be no fire in the mornin' and if they ain't no fire in the mornin', they won't be no breakfast in the mornin'." (Without fail, the wood box got filled every night.)

We toted water from the spring: two buckets at a time, (which took half as many trips and we could almost walk level.) With all the cooking, canning, washing dishes and bathing we did, that too was a full time job. Warren and I would've been a foot taller if we hadn't worn our legs off totin' all that water. As time passed, the spring path became a knee-deep rut; partly caused by erosion, but mostly caused by totin' water for so many years. As the rut wore deeper, our legs got shorter and the buckets dragged on the ground. I figure our well came along at just the right time.

The first warm days of spring were perfect for running expeditions on Stewart's Creek, but it didn't work that way on our hill; as the world warmed up, we headed for the fields and almost lived there. All that work had to be done, not tomorrow, not next week, but "right now boys, while the sun shines." We plowed the land, sowed the seeds, cultivated, hoed and harvested, while being constantly told, "Anybody around here wants anything to eat this winter besides snowballs is gonna' help grow it." I helped.

Come spring and summer, we picked, dug, broke, peeled, dried and canned everything in sight. I don't know how many canning jars Mama had, but there were many and she filled every one every summer. She did most of the canning in the washtub over an outdoor fire, which took even more wood. I figured if we didn't slack off soon, there'd soon be no more trees and no more Great North Woods left to explore. One family in the neighborhood had already burned every tree on their small farm, so it could happen.

All spring and summer, we lived in the fields: plowing and hoeing corn, hoeing, suckering and worming tobacco. In late summer, we primed and cured tobacco, pulled fodder, cut corn tops and had more to do than twenty people could do and it wouldn't get any better any time soon.

Just like the Indians, we spent the whole summer getting ready for winter. Unlike us, they didn't stay in one place for a lifetime and had no need for big fields. They could move on at will and never had to hoe a hundred miles of cornrows in the boiling sun. Why, oh why, couldn't I have been an Indian?

Some lucky farmers owned creek bottoms that were level, had soft dirt that was easy to plow and hoe and even in dry spells, corn grew well there. As Pa said it, "Corn grows so big in them bottoms, you hafta' climb the stalk to get a "roasneer." We never owned any but sharecropped five different bottoms along Stewart's Creek at various times. If our rocky fields had been creek bottoms, we'd have been millionaires ten times over.

Not only did we sharecrop the five bottoms, but every other field Pa could find. At one time or another, we almost lived in the up-land fields of Grandpa, Dan Hawks, Walter Marshall, Sid Marshall and Linc Gardner. Throw in our own fields and that didn't leave many. Some of the fields were full of rocks, which were inedible and didn't sell very well, but we grew corn there without fail.

As sure as the sun came up in spring, it was a sure bet we'd be in a field somewhere and we'd be there "before the crow peed." We plowed, hoed, sweated, cussed and drank the water jug dry. It took forever for the sun to crawl cross the sky and some days, I thought it would never go down behind the mountain.

Everything we planted did well, because a certain person with a hickory switch kept certain people pulling weeds and hoeing. "Boy, you lean on that hoe handle long enough, it's gonna' sprout and grow and when it does, you ain't gonna' have nothin' left to set' on when I git done with your hide." I could see it on my tombstone: "Here lies Mr Easter: master weed-puller."

On occasion, Pa made moonshine from our corn meal and a good rain made the corn crop look promising, which made the moonshine crop look promising. He was known to brew up a batch and was always in a good mood after a summer rain. In all the years I was home, we never had a corn crop failure and Pa never had a moonshine failure.

We also had no garden failures, because he kept an eagle eye on everything. He set a mole trap to catch "them plowing up every thing in sight varmints" and sometimes caught one. In late evenings, he stood watch with his single-shot Iver Johnson twenty-gauge shotgun and tried to shoot the rabbits that were "eatin' up everything them damn moles ain't already plowed up." Without the shotgun and mole trap, we would've died on the vine, long before I ever "growed up."

After a good rain, gardens, crops and grass and weeds, especially weeds, grew "wide open" twenty-four hours a day. Cornstalks headed for the sky and pumpkin and watermelon vines headed for the hills. As the old timers said it, "Them vines growed so fast, they drug the bottoms plumb offa' the watermelons and punkins' and we had run 'em down and cut the ends off. We got plumb tired tryin' to run them things down all over the place. Got tangled up in a vine one time and might near choked to death. Them was dangerous times, let me tell you."

When a thunderstorm ran Stewart's Creek muddy, normal sensible people went cat fishing, but there were no such people at our house. After windy storms, we headed for the muddy fields and set tobacco and corn stalks back up straight by packing mud around them with our bare feet. We sawed flue wood in the South Forty Woods and toted wash water and re-sprayed the bean vines. Again, an opinion from the old folks, "Way back yonder, we didn't hafta' do all that spraying and stuff to grow a good garden. All we had to do was stick some seeds in the ground and git the heck out of the way."

Our only saving grace was the rare occasion when a thunderstorm came and we had no jobs waiting. The walking dead instantly came to life and we headed for far places. With the whole big woods to prowl, mountains to climb and fish to catch, Heaven help anybody or anything that got in our way.

Pa liked to fish too and when a storm ran the creek muddy, he sometimes couldn't help himself and we went fishing. We dug fish worms, cut fishing poles from Oscar Marshall's Woods and raced to the Abe Hole: hoping the catfish would be jumping out on the bank, be as big as a "baccer setter" and hungry as a wolf.

Everybody tried to get there first, bait a hook and start fishing first. There was no better feeling than sitting on the creek bank watching the muddy creek roll by: hoping to catch the biggest catfish anybody ever seen. With the land too wet to plow, maybe, just maybe, we could go fishing again tomorrow.

Looking west on the overgrown Cleve Thomas Road (1971)

    The early morning dew was cold on bare feet as we followed the horse and sled east along the Cleve Thomas Road. With hoes on shoulders, we marched like soldiers going to war and by the end of the day; we'd feel and look like we'd fought one. Grandpa's hillside pasture was on the left side of the road. (Seen on the right above in 1971; looking in the opposite direction and grown up in trees.) His cow wore a bell that could almost always be heard when walking along the road.

    A drawbar pasture gate blocked the road beside an old sawmill place, with poplar trees on both sides. The pasture fence curved left around the hill and continued almost to Stewart's Creek. A path crossed the fence that led up to Grandpa's rocky cornfield on top of the hill. It was a great downhill shortcut when going fishing at the Abe Hole, but a long hard climb going back up.

    Beyond the pasture gate, wild strawberries, dewberries, blackberries and sassafras bushes grew on both sides of the road, as it continued into Grandpa's bottom. Smooth water-worn creek rocks grew in a small upper area and more came up after every rain. There were more than an army could pick up and a huge pile beside the road grew bigger every year. Plowing in the rocky area was hard work and Pa spoke some strange words as the plow bounced and clanged along. (His language may have been why corn didn't grow well there.)

    The rock pile was a great place to play and the "biggest and best blackberries anybody ever seen" grew around it. We were warned, "They's copperheads hidin' in there biggern' you are and they don't like kids a'tall." When nobody was looking, we played on the rock pile, ate the berries and hunted for snakes.

    The sun was just coming up over Dave Carson's bottoms, as we began plowing and hoeing corn in Grandpa's bottom. Pa plowed with the five-point cultivator and Old John, as (in his own words) he "follered the south end of a horse headed north all day long." We followed along behind and chopped cockle-burrs, horse nettles and ragweed and pulled dirt around the cornstalks. As the sun climbed higher, the day got hotter and the fresh-plowed dirt felt cool on hot bare feet.

    As the day dragged on, it got hotter, we got hotter and the long rows got longer and "reached from one end to the other." On the longest rows, we passed ourselves coming back. Some days, the sun stood still in the sky, just like it did in the bible. But somehow, some way, we always made it back home, rested all night and come next day, we did it all over again.

    We plowed, chopped, hoed and sweated our life away in Grandpa's bottom, while Stewart's Creek sang a fishing song as it splashed down over the rapids at the Spruce Pine Hole. It might as well have been in another county, because there'd be no wading or fishing on corn-hoeing days. What good was a creek nobody had time to play in?

Grandpa's Bottom: looking west from Stewart's Creek in 1971: with Fisher's Peak in the far background.

We didn't need a water jug while working in Grandpa's bottom, because of a spring that came from under a huge rock in the bluff. (At left above.) When we got too hot, we took a break, drank the cold water, cooled our feet in the spring branch and sat in the shade of poplar trees to cool and "rest our weary bones." On the hottest days, we almost drank the spring dry.

The Cleve Thomas Road continued through the middle of the bottom (from center to right above) to a ford beside the High Foot Log. Beyond the creek, the road climbed up-hill by the Harvey Lee and Virginia Thomas house and continued to the Cleve Thomas place.

On another day, we hoed corn in Grandpa's rocky hilltop field mentioned before. Far down in the valley, Stewart's Creek shimmered brightly in the morning sun, as we chopped weeds and hoed corn and rocks. All the while, the water jug and my younger brothers sat on an old quilt in the shade of an oak tree.

Again, Pa spoke some strange words as he plowed the rocky field. Meanwhile, Warren and I checked out Newton's theory of gravity and rolled some of the rocks downhill through the pasture into the Cleve Thomas Road. Sure enough, every one of them rolled downhill and lucky for us, nobody got rock-bombed.

When crows pulled up new corn plants in spring, Pa shot one and hung it from the top of a tall pole to keep other crows away and when the corn ears matured, he repeated the process. If that didn't work, he went to Plan B and mounted a steel trap on top of the pole. When a crow landed in the trap, it made so much noise; every other crow in the country flew in to see what was wrong. Together, they made so much noise; everybody knew Pa had caught another crow.

Everything raided cornfields: coons, crows, stray cows, horses, mules, squirrels and sometimes a hungry traveler. While running important backwoods missions, a certain famous scout sometimes staved off starvation by raiding a neighbor's cornfield for a "roasneer." With corn growing all over the country, nobody cared if an ear or two disappeared, especially for a good cause. Pa solved most of the varmint problems with his shotgun, but made an exception for a hungry son; no way would he shoot his best weed-puller.

Wild 'simmons (persimmons) and wild plums grew along the split rail fence and big sour blackberries grew in a small hollow at the west end. The biggest berries were always the sourest, but sold just like small ones and filled the bucket much faster. More blackberries and dewberries grew along the rail fence and field edges. We only tended the rocky field for one year and like so many other worn-out fields, it finally grew up in broom straw.

On another summer morning, we rolled out early to hoe tobacco in Grandpa's field beside the Sawmill Road. The dew-covered grass was cold on bare feet, but as the sun climbed higher, so did the temperature and by mid-morning, Fisher's Peak was shimmering in the west, with not a cloud in sight.

We'd already been working in the hot fields for days on end and I was brain-cooked, probably beyond hope. As the morning dragged on, we plowed and dug and dug some more. All the while, Pa and Grandpa kept an eye on the sky, watching for signs of a shower. That made no sense when all I could see up there was a burning sun and a mountain about to melt. I knew it would never rain again and we'd probably be hoeing tobacco for the rest of our lives, if we lived that long.

Even the signs were wrong, because the moon was crescent shaped with the tips pointed up, which meant, according to Grandpa, it would catch any rain that tried to fall. (When the tips were pointed down, it meant "she's gonna' pour it all out, boys, right here right here on top of us, ker' splash.")

I checked my special edition mail-order wind-up pocket watch to see if it was still running. It was, but in low gear, like its owner. An hour later, it had only moved five minutes and at that rate, dinnertime would never come. We took a break in the shade, while Old John stood in the sun with his head hung down: looking like he was on his last legs. Even the plow looked tired.

I knew for a fact, if things didn't change soon, they'd have to bury me right there in the field. I'd heard of an unmarked grave somewhere along the Sawmill Road and who ever was buried there probably died from working in the hot sun, just like somebody else was about to. If I became the second person to die in the same field, we both would become famous.

The water jug ran dry early, but somehow we made it until dinnertime and took a two-hour break in the heat of the day. Like always, Grandpa curled up in the floor with his arm under his head for a pillow and took a nap. He soon woke up again raring to go, but his grandson was never that eager. All too soon we were right back out there: digging in the hot sun again: hotter than ever.

Storm clouds over Fisher's Peak

Just as I was preparing to meet my Maker, clouds began climbing into the sky over Fisher's Peak. "Look back yonder; I think it's a' comin' up a storm." It was beyond belief as more and more clouds filled the western sky, all the way from Fisher's Peak to Sugar Loaf Mountain. When thunder began toward Galax, Pa said, "That's the bread wagon comin' our way, boys and she's gonna' come a good 'un. Them taters'll grow so fast, they'll jump right outta' the ground and them corn stalks'll grow so big, we'll hafta' cut 'em down with the cross-cut saw."

As the sky got darker, the thunder got louder and in spite of all my doubts and fears, rain was coming for sure and maybe, just maybe, we'd get a break from the burning fields. Maybe, just maybe, the creek would run muddy and we could go cat fishing.

When rain came over Fisher's Peak, we headed home and got there just as the first big drops stirred up dust in the front yard. They plopped loudly on the tin roof and harder rain came down the hill, roared on the tin roof and chilled the air that had been so hot just a short time ago.

Lightning lit up the dark room, thunder rattled the windows and I jumped plumb out of my skin. "That'n struck right here close, boys." As a neighbor told us about another storm, "It poured like pouring water out of a bucket right here on top of us, then it moved off down yonder way and turned right around and come back and poured some more. It looked like it was never gonna' quit and I ain't never seen so much rain before no how. Now that was a rain to end all rains, I'm here to tell you."

Our dog howled from under the house: reminding me of a neighbor boy who hid under the kitchen table when he heard thunder. We were not exactly afraid of storms but knew better than to go outside during a bad one. The last thing I needed was to get fried like fatback, as lightning was said to do.

A flood poured off the front porch roof and a muddy river ran down the road: both headed for Stewart's Creek. Another muddy river ran downhill through the pasture and Pa said, "There goes the baccer' patch right down the holler."

The storm moved "on east," the sun came back and everything smelled fresh, cool and clean. A rainbow over the barn showed us where a pot of gold was buried. "All you gotta' do is git to the end of it and dig it up." (We tried, but the ends always moved before we got there.)

With no crops blown over by the wind, there'd be no more work in the fields that day. How in the world could we ever survive such a problem? Since it had also rained around Lambsburg, we knew Stewart's Creek would soon be running red-muddy and to ease our misery, we dug fish worms and went cat fishing.

Growing tobacco was man-killing work, much more so than corn. When sarvice' (service) trees bloomed in February, we grubbed new plant beds from the woods, sowed tobacco seeds, covered the beds with plant bed cloth and watered them if it didn't rain.

As winter went back over the mountain, Pa "turned the land " with Old John and a hillside turning plow. He then harrowed the fields with the "harr" (harrow) to break up clods and make the land smooth. When ready to set the tobacco plants, he "layed off" rows across the fields and we scattered fertilizer in them from a peck bucket. He then covered it with the plow and we set tobacco plants.

When the plants began growing, that's when the fun began and we spent the better part of every spring and summer in the tobacco fields trying to keep up. We babied the plants, plowed, hoed, wormed, topped, suckered, set them back up if the wind blew them down, cussed them and sweated blood.

The hard work continued until the plants grew so big the leaves broke off while working around them. Foxhounds sometimes, ran through the fields and did some early priming and that's when Pa threatened to go foxhunter hunting.

Finally at long last, came an annual ritual almost as good as Foot Washing Day at Crooked Oak Church. We gave thanks to the Gods and "laid the tobacco fields by." It was one of the best times of summer, because there'd be no more work there until priming time. There was no better feeling than walking out of a tobacco field for the last time, headed for home with a worn-out hoe on a worn-out shoulder.

We almost lived on corn: we ate it in the young "roasneer" stage, ground it into corn meal to make bread and fed it to the animals and chickens. Some of it became the main ingredient in moonshine far in the backwoods.

The Easters had grown corn exactly the same way, ever since Columbus headed west. When signs were in the head, we turned the land, harrowed it to death and made rows across it with the lay-off plow. "If them rows ain't straight, boy, they ain't no use in plantin' no corn 'cause it ain't gonna' grow right,"

We planted cornfields when white oak leaves became the size of a squirrel's ear, everywhere Pa found some dirt. He "laid-off" rows with the lay-off plow and we dropped a small amount of fertilizer where a hill was to be. "Put two grains of corn beside the fertilizer, but "not on it" and cover it up with the hoe: "not too deep and don't put no clods on top."

As the corn came up, crows began pulling it out of the ground to eat the grain of seed corn. That's when Pa "put some more lead in some more hides" with his shotgun. As it grew, we prayed for rain, because unlike the garden and tobacco fields, corn didn't fare well during a drought. (No matter what the weather, weeds headed for the sky anytime.)

To let a cornfield grow up in weeds was a social disaster of the first order and we plowed and hoed them three times a season. We piled dirt around the stalks and woe unto a weed that dared to come up in early summer. Despite hail, windstorms, marauding animals and other bothers, we never had a corn crop failure.

Finally at long last, another hallowed day came and we "laid the cornfields by." Finally at long last, we had some free time again and we tried to make the most of it. The walking dead came to life as we headed for the great outdoors to fish, hunt, wade, explore and do whatever came to mind. No matter what the weather, it was never too hot to play.

There were two big problems with fishing in mid-summer: the water was so hot the fish wouldn't bite and the fish worms had gone to China. On top of that, a green slime covered everything in the creek. "Don't you go wadin' down yonder in that green stuff, boys. It'll eat your toes off and you'll catch no tellin' what." When we finally had some free time, we could neither fish, wade nor swim, so why even have a creek?

Warren and I made a tent from Mama's worn-out kitchen tablecloth and set it up in the woods below the spring. It was a great place to camp in the daytime and almost as much fun as wading and fishing. Pa said he thought a family of Gypsies had moved in down on the branch.

We planned to rough it and camp there all night, until he told us, "They's Haints out there in them woods at night, boys and Old Blind Topsy (who had died years ago) still gits' somebody ever now and then." Not that we were afraid or anything, but I did wonder how fast she could run, being blind and all that. Even though we were fearless, we just never quite got around to camping anywhere overnight.

It took three things to become a good whittler: a sharp Barlow knife, a piece of wood and the ability to "spit good." The way it worked, the better you could spit, the better you could whittle and vice versa and it took years of practice. The old folks "chawed 'baccer," spit way out yonder, whittled out walking canes, axe handles, singletrees, solved all of the world's problems, told us about the good old days and spit some more.

The way they told it, "The way we growed up back yonder, you boys don't know how good you got it. You live on easy street, ridin' them bicycles and all that. Back in our day, it snowed so much we never seen no ground from November 'til March and it was all uphill, ever' which-a-way we went; goin' and comin' back too. Made you tired after a while: climbing uphill all the time in all that snow and we didn't have no bicycles. My old legs was a foot longer 'afore I wore 'em off."

We never "chawed baccer," but we learned to whittle and spit anyway. We made bows and arrows, windmills, zizz wheels and thing-a-ma-jigs. We whittled initials on trees, skinned rabbits and squirrels, cut fishing poles, cleaned fish, peeled apples, trimmed broken toenails and made blow guns. "Always whittle away from yourself, boys, and you wont get hurt."

We made corncob pipes and smoked everything in sight: rabbit tobacco, oak leaves and corn silks. When we tried real tobacco, faces turned green, the world turned upside down and stomachs turned "wrong-side-outards." We decided right away: grownups could keep their real 'baccer. We fought World War Two with corncobs and held Wild West shootouts. Nobody got hurt with corncobs, which were safer than the rocks some kids threw at each other.

We made "zizz wheels" from a big button and a piece of string that pulled your hair out when they got tangled up in it. It was very hard to unwind everything without a sizable hair loss. "If you don't wanta' look like the moon comin' up, keep them zizz wheels away from your head. You gonna' look funny runnin' around here without no hair."

We learned to get a silver dollar rolling around the inside wall of Mama's dishpan. There was a certain knack to it; you had to hold your mouth just right, get a good grip on your tongue and look at it squench-eyed. After some heavy practice, Warren and I both became expert dish-panners.

People did the same type of thing at the fair, as they rode motorcycles around the inside of circular walls made for the purpose. One man didn't even hold onto the handlebars and stood up as he rode around and around inside the wall.

An old bicycle wheel with no tire and a yard-long stick became a new mode of transportation we drove for miles. After getting the wheel rolling along, just pushing it with a stick took us all over the place. Throwing in a few motorized sounds made it work even better, especially when pulling a big load uphill. Our dog liked driving too and ran along behind us, barking all the way. The old timers told about kids making motor noises while pushing a block of wood around in the dirt: many years before cars were invented.

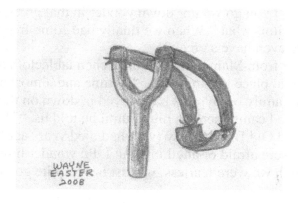

"Our high-powered weepon"

We made slingshots from "Y" shaped ivy limbs, old shoe leather and strips of rubber from a worn-out inner tube. (Seen above.) We heard the usual static, "Them things is high powered weepons' boys and you gonna' put your eyes out." Everything we liked or did was dangerous to eyes and limbs and most likely, we'd be blind in both eyes and lame to boot: long before we ever "growed up."

My slingshot was no threat to animals and birds, but anything that made a noise when hit with a rock was another story. Barn sides, tin roofs, stray dogs and Mama's washtub lived a hard life. The washtub made the best noise but she promised us bodily if I shot it again.

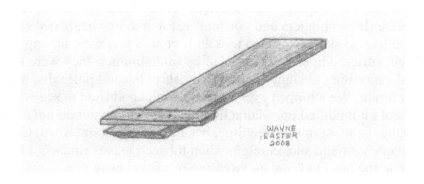

The Lizard

We made a "Lizard" from a four-foot piece of plank and rode it down a steep wooded hillside on Jim's Knob. The more we rode it, the slicker the bottom became and the faster it went. It was our most exciting game, but nobody had enough nerve to ride it all the way down the hill. When it got up too much speed, we just flopped off sideways into the leaves and tried to miss logs and trees. Then we walked to the bottom of the knob to find it, made the long climb back uphill and did it all over again. Nobody worried about breaking limbs or bashing heads against trees, because such things never happened to good kids like us.

Warren and I dreamed up some world-changing projects, but most were never finished. I bought a ten-cent can of bent nails at a farm auction and we dived into another major deal. We cut small saplings, built a playhouse and used up almost all of the nails.

When we got four walls built, a floor, a hole in the wall for a window and another for a door, we quit. (Who needed a roof anyway?) It was at least 50 feet from home and a great place to camp in the daytime, but when the sun went down, nobody or nothing would catch *us* out there in the dark; we headed for home.

We were warned about lightning, "That's dangerous stuff, boys. You see a storm comin', you head home and if you see you can't make it, stay away from them trees, 'bob wire fences and fields." (Best I could tell; that didn't leave anywhere else to go.) I'd already seen trees that lightning had blown apart and when thunder began, I headed for home.

It was a known fact that burning lightning-struck trees for firewood would bring the worst kind of luck and might even burn your house down. Pa's take on the subject, "Ain't nobody burnin' no lightnin'-struck wood on this hill." Nobody did.

Mama made jams, jellies and pies from blackberries and we sold some at Rossie Golding's Store on Lambsburg Road. Picking blackberries was almost fun, until some small dot-sized varmints called chiggers began eating me alive. They lived on berry vines and could hardly wait to ambush their favorite person. Soon after biting, they started itching and I was soon "all eat up, all over."

Pa didn't pick blackberries, because he had more important things to do like running the farm and shooting the shotgun. Grapes were a whole different story and both he and Grandpa made grape wine. Grandpa stored his in kegs in the smokehouse, but Pa's wine didn't hang around long enough to store.

Fleas were another disaster and if one came within a mile, it nailed me, made a huge bump and itched worse than chiggers. Given a choice between a dog and me; a flea would bite me every time. The same was true with ticks and the scary thing about *them*: they ate on you for a while before you knew anything about it.

We never got snake-bit, lightning struck and no trees fell on us, but we tangled with yellow jackets, hornets, ticks, fleas, chiggers and poison ivy. Such things happened to anyone who ran wild in the woods; if you had no skins, stumped toes and bruises, you were having no fun at all.

Tender bare feet suffered in early spring, but by mid-summer, they were tough enough to stomp rocks. We stomped everything in sight: including mushrooms and puffballs, but best of all was a mud hole just after a rain. We stomped every one we found and tried to see who could stomp the biggest. When we got all muddied up, Mama threatened to stomp a mud hole in us.

We tried to make the most of our free time, because all too soon, it would come to a screeching halt. It happened every year and sure enough, when tobacco leaves ripened, playtime was over and we were right back in the hot fields again, sweating our lives away.

We primed tobacco leaves off the stalks, hauled them to the barn, twined them on sticks and hung them in the barn. If a thunderstorm came, we had to stop until it was over and sometimes finished up late, sometimes by lantern light well after dark. Some days were so long, I thought suppertime would never come.

After the tobacco yellowed for a few days, Pa fired the barn flues heavily: keeping in mind the fine balance between keeping the tobacco at the right temperature and burning the barn down. Flue wood vanished by the cord and as the saying went, "With a little bit of luck, a barn full of wood just might cure a barn full of tobacco sometimes, maybe."

He kept the fires burning twenty-four hours a day and caught catnaps at night. I stayed all night too and roasted 'roasneers, potatoes and apples in the flue fires and checked the temperature inside the barn. I also slept well in a tobacco sled in the wee hours, knowing snakes couldn't get inside. Next day, we were right back in the fields again.

After the tobacco was cured, the process of storing, "ordering" and tying it began. Finally at long last, we sold it at the warehouses in Mt. Airy. Selling was what tobacco was all about and after "paying-up" Kasco's Feed and Seed store, we still had money and after going barefoot all summer, Warren and I got new shoes.

When all of the tobacco was primed off the stalks, I worked out a whole summer's frustrations chopping them down with a tobacco knife. When finished, that field no longer existed. "You be careful, boy! Them 'baccer-knives'll cut your legs off."

Corn shocks

With the coming of August, we were right back in the cornfields again, pulling fodder and cutting tops. On rare occasions, we cut the entire cornstalks off at the ground and stacked them into shocks that looked like rows of Indian teepees standing across the field. After they dried, we hauled them home, pulled the ears off and fed the rest to the animals.

Instead of shocking the corn, we normally pulled fodder (the leaves below the corn ears) off the stalk, tied it in bundles and hung them on the corn ears to dry. When the wind blew them down, we hung them back up and when completely dry, they became winter food for the horse and cow.

We later cut the corn tops (the cornstalk and leaves *above* the ears.) and tied them in bundles around another corn stalk to dry. That left the half-stalks standing with an ear or two of corn at the top. When the tops had dried, they too became animal food. With a barn full of fodder and tops, the horse and cow were all fixed up for winter.

Finally at long last, we pulled the ears of corn off the stalks, hauled them home in Grandpa's wagon and dumped them in a huge pile in the middle of the road. I never heard a reason for doing so: it was just the way the Easters did it, another one of many things I didn't understand. When anything or anybody came along, they found a huge pile of corn in the middle of the road and had to detour around it.

On corn-shucking day, neighbors gathered in, shucked the corn, told tall tales, forecasted the weather and swapped the latest gossip. The favor was returned until everybody's corn was shucked and stored in the owner's corncrib or granary. Sometimes a jug of moonshine was found near the bottom of the corn piles and the shucks really flew.

The women cooked a big "corn shucking" dinner and nobody went home hungry. When all of our corn was shucked, the road was again open to traffic until next year. With a granary full of corn, a barn full of tops and fodder and a basement full of can-stuff, everybody and everything was ready and waiting for winter.

The very hardest jobs, like corn shuckings, house and barn raisings were done with the help of neighbors. They helped each other in times of need, as neighborhood women did the housework work and the men tended crops, cut firewood and cared for the animals.

When someone died, neighbors dug a grave with hand tools, made a casket of pine boards and the deceased was prepared for burial. People brought in food, held an all-night wake and next day, the deceased was hauled to the church by horse and wagon to lie in state, the funeral was preached and burial followed in the church cemetery.

Hard work was the way of life on Stewart's Creek and if it had been harmful, no one would've been left alive by years end. Even so, some of the best farming took place as neighbors sat on the front porch and talked about the weather and other neighbors.

Self-reliance was how it was done and every family handled their own problems as best they could. When something broke, they repaired it with whatever was handy: a piece of wire, twine, pocketknife, hammer, axe, a few choice words and a shot of moonshine. When an ax or mattock handle broke, they whittled a new one from a white oak or hickory sapling. I remember my grandfather's worn-out leather harness he'd used for many years. From necessity and lack of money, it had been repaired many times with wire and string, but it still worked.

Farmer's wives were the hardest workers of all; they worked in the fields, canned food for winter, kept house, tended kids, patched and mended clothes, doctored the sick and cooked three meals a day every day of the year. With so many jobs that absolutely had to be done right now, today: jobs that only they could do, there was no time to be sick or out of sorts and they did them without fail.

Mama was one of those and in the early years, she sometimes made do with almost nothing. She "rolled out" dough for biscuits and pies with a glass bottle, until she whittled a real rolling pin from a sourwood sapling. (Seen on the following page.) Rumor had it that she may have cleaned house with it on occasion, as Pa did with the shotgun. Between the two, we probably had the cleanest house in the whole county.

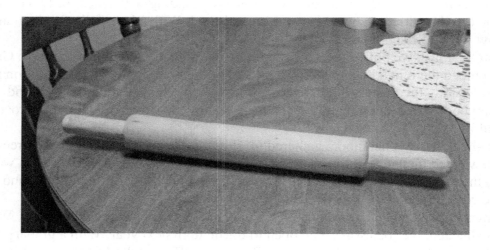

Mama's sourwood rolling pin (2009)

Pa's axe   Our axe

Part 5

At home in Toast N C. March 1960

Icicles on the Blue Ridge Parkway (1971)

Chapter 13

Winter

The Third Knob and Fisher's Peak

Thanksgiving and Christmas were already gone and a brand new year was coming from "just over that mountain back yonder," bringing the big snows of January. That's what winter was all about and according to Pa, "They improve the land, improve your health and kill a whole buncha' them varmints." (Even after the worst winters, we never had a shortage of varmints, because chiggers, fleas, ticks and mosquitoes ate me alive every summer.)

The old timers could tell when weather was coming by watching the sky, "That sun she's a wadin' snow back yonder, boy, and she'll be coming over that mountain 'afore mornin'. These here old bones is a' achin' bad, so git in plenty a' wood, cause it's gonna' come a big 'un."

One of the few things Pa and Mama agreed on, "It's gonna' snow" and my whole family looked forward to the big ones. Our roads became impassable, but with no car, we hadn't planned on going anywhere anyhow.

It was said mules could smell rain coming and I could almost for sure, smell snow coming. When I mentioned that little fact to Pa, he said, "What you're smellin', boy, is your upper lip." (I don't think he understood us scientific types.)

Most of the old folks didn't share my enthusiasm, "When you've seen as many snows as I have, boy, you won't like 'em neither. Way back yonder, we never seen no ground from November 'til March and we waded snow plumb up to here. On top a' that, we run plumb outta' wood one winter and might near froze to death."

Sounds traveled far in the cold air just before a snowfall and there was a roar high in the sky. We could hear big trucks climbing Fancy Gap Mountain ten miles away, foxhounds running in the Gardner Woods and neighbors chopping wood in Hoot Owl Holler'. Every animal and bird knew snow was coming and ate everything in sight, just like Warren and I did every day.

We banged the house doors all day long as we ran in and out: hoping to catch that first snowflake on our tongues, "Catch that first one and you'll have extra good luck." With a buckeye and a rabbit's foot on hand, I had the luck thing pretty well sewed up, but just in case, I too, caught some first snowflakes.

When snow was coming, I kept an eye on Fisher's Peak, because most of our weather came from that direction. When I saw it come over Bald Rock, I could, almost without fail, predict snow in the immediate future.

"High thin clouds"

    After some cold sunny days in a brand new year, high thin clouds climbed into the western sky. As the day wore on, they thickened; chased away the sun and the whole world became smooth-cloudy. Summer was only a memory as we settled in for a long siege. With a stack of firewood, fatback in the granary, corn meal and flour in the meal chest, walnuts in the granary, apples and canned stuff in the basement, we were ready. With a gallon of kerosene on hand, a lamp to read by and books from the school library, I was ready too. (No way could anybody make it through a big snow without books.)

    We toted extra water from the spring, because mushing two full buckets uphill in knee-deep snow was almost impossible. Sliding downhill was easy, but sliding back up was when the fun began. We did the chores early, ate supper and kept a snow-watch going by shining Pa's flashlight up into the black sky. "You all run my new bat'trys' down, I'm gonna' have me some hide:" a threat we heard often. We finally gave up, went to bed and somehow, someway, far in the night, we slept.

"The old woman pluckin' her geese up yonder"

    When Pa called next morning, he told us, "Git outta' that bed, boys. The Old Woman, she's a "pluckin' her geese up yonder and she's a stickin'." Sure enough, huge snowflakes were falling and the ground was already white. "Wonder how much we gonna' get, It ain't gonna' quit yet is it? Huh? Huh? Think it'll come a big 'un?"

118

As snow kept falling, Pa manned the yardstick and thermometer and fired the wood heater "as hot as she'll run." The stovepipe turned cherry red all the way to the flue, as he sat close in his favorite chair and smoked "roll your own" Golden Grain cigarettes. He told us once again, "Ain't nobody never gonna' be cold in this house as long as the wood holds out."

We broke new trails to the barn, the chicken house and the granary, fed the animals and milked the cow. We built snowmen and igloos; shook snow off sagging pine limbs and tried to roll snowballs down the pasture hill. When thoroughly frozen, we tracked snow into the house and crowded around the heater. Mama said, "You-all clean them feet off before you come in here." (Just like mud, could I help it if snow followed me home?) When thawed out and re-fueled, back again we went to the great outdoors.

With a dishpan of snow, milk, sugar and vanilla flavoring, Mama made snow cream, while Pa "parched" peanuts in the oven and kept an eye on the cook stove. Only the nimble-footed could raise the lids, peek in the pots and stay out of Mama's way. With so many years of practice under his belt, he had it down to a science and could peep and dodge with the best.

Mama was a great cook and never failed to have our meals ready: even when tired, didn't feel well, or didn't have much food on hand. (In later years, she told us there were times when we had almost nothing to eat for the next meal, but suppertime always came.)

Even on ordinary days, nobody had to be told to gather around the table at meal times; it was the most popular place in the house. On snowy days it was a dangerous place, because working a big snow created big appetites. We'd had nothing to eat for at least an hour, starvation was at hand and it was a catfight to get to the table without a collision. "You young-uns' behave or I'll throw the whole mess outn' the yard." (Truth be known, food didn't hang around our house long enough to throw anywhere.)

In late day, the snow quit falling, the temperature went down and the wind came up. Pa said, "She's gonna' be a rough un' out there tonight, boys; git everything done early." We re-stocked the wood box, milked the cow, fed the animals and ate supper. After a hard day at the mines, we went to bed "with the chickens" and daydreamed of all the places we'd go tomorrow in the new snow. It had been one heck of a good day and tomorrow would be just as good, maybe better. When the sandman finally came, we went to dreamland and slept the whole night through.

Tracking in new snow

We hit the trail early next day with mission clear: "track them rabbits." Armed with dog, slingshots, telescope and peanuts, we rambled all over "you know where and half a' Georgia" as Pa said it. We found dog, fox and rabbit tracks in the snow, but never saw the first wild animal. I figured two ace scouts could track something down, especially with the best rabbit dog in the country, but the only thing it tracked was *us* as it followed along behind.

We telescoped the white-trimmed mountainsides, hoping to see one of "Danl' Boone's bars'," or at least "one of them wild mountain goats" said to be there. We never saw the first living thing, wild or otherwise in the mountainside, or anywhere else for that matter.

Cold was no problem early on and we tramped for hours in the great outdoors. When the peanuts ran out and we got cold, tired minds turned to a warm house and a warm supper. Having had no luck in the tracking department, we headed down the long trail home. "We'll get them rabbits tomorrow when they're hungrier."

With three-foot icicles hanging from the roof, the windows frosted up and snow still on the ground, we figured winter had come for sure. We learned how wrong that was a few days later when one of Grandpa's "old timey ice storms" came raging down from the mountain.

From straight out of Bobbitt Holler' "she" came, wide open with teeth and claws, driven by a screaming wind that threw wind-snow sideways. In dark north-facing bluffs, green laurel leaves curled up into round tubes from the cold and Stewart's Creek froze solid. Nights outside were deadly and they came early in the cold hard days of January.

Survival was a matter of shelter, firewood, heavy quilts and last summer's food stored in the cellar. We stuffed rags and newspapers in door and window cracks to keep out the wind. "Shut that door, younguns'. You gonna' freeze us all to death. Was you raised in a barn?"

The warmest place in the house was beside the red-hot heater and there we stayed until bedtime. Mama then piled every quilt we had on the beds. "If we don't freeze to death first, we gonna' smother under all that cover." We dived into ice-cold beds and shivered until we got warm, then slept the whole night through. Come next morning, Pa re-fired the heater, broke ice in the water buckets and we shivered again until we got warm.

Except for the normal everyday chores, our world was reduced to four walls and a window. "Anybody with any sense 'a-tall don't go prowling around out yonder after dark. You git lost out there in this kinda' weather, boy, you gonna' be a goner."

From far down in a dull sky, winter's sun warmed other people in other lands, as cold "like nobody ever seen before" settled into the high hills and deep valleys. We were socked in close and it was hard to remember warm weather. Worst of all: there would be no more backwoods missions until better weather.

Being afraid of falling on the ice and breaking something, the old folks stayed by the fire and dreamed of yesterday and warmer times in other years. Warren and I had no such problems; no way could we break anything, we'd probably live forever and could hardly wait to get out there and slide on the ice.

Nothing but a few trees and a bob' wire fence stood between our house and Sugar Loaf Mountain and we were right in the line of fire. When the sun went down, so did the thermometer, then the wind came up: the kind that blew away barn doors. Then the bottom fell out of everything.

We did the chores early, ate supper, went to bed and listened to the wind. All night long, it rattled our windows and broke our woods. Next morning, Pa told us, "She'd a' blowed much harder last night, boys, she'd a' blowed us plumb offa' this ridge and we'd a' been livin' down yonder in the holler'." There was no longer any doubt in anybody's mind: winter had come for sure, it had come to stay and we were right in the middle of "the coldest time I ever seen."

The wind was a strange sucker: you could feel it, hear it, it could blow you away and certain people like Pa could "see it coming." It almost never quit in winter and when it did, we could still hear it roaring in the mountain. Everybody said, "That wind, she blows harder right here at our house than anywhere else in the world and she drives everybody mad."

I watched black crows fly to a standstill against high headwinds. They hung there for a few seconds, then veered off and flew back the way they came. Brothers "Orville and Wilbur" Easter, tried to get a homemade kite into the air, but when the string broke, it landed in a pine tree and stayed there. (I tried and tried, but never saw the wind.)

A snowy Sugar Loaf Mountain

Sometime in the night, the storm "moved on east" and we woke up to a sunny, shiny frozen world. After being cooped up for days on end, everything looked brand new. A deep blue, trimmed-in-white Sugar Loaf Mountain stood high over Little Sid Marshall's house and pink clouds raced south across the sky as they tried to outrun the cold.

The sun-lit ice was blinding and hard to walk on when one foot went northwest and the other went southeast. Every step made a crunching sound and cracks in the ice coat raced away into the woods. With our help, huge pieces of ice rattled and slid all the way down the pasture hill. "You youngun's stay offa' them icy hillsides or you gonna' wind up hurt down yonder in the holler'."

Grandpa's snowplow

During big snows, Grandpa scraped our road with his homemade horse-drawn snowplow. It looked like a big letter "A" and he rode on top to hold it down as the horse pulled it along the road. It made zig-zag path, but we could then mush to his house without wading deep snow.

Ground Hog Day came and went and nothing changed except the weather and the woodpile: one got colder and the other got smaller. The days raced by wide open, but the long dark nights dragged on forever in the deepest, darkest, coldest part of winter.

Heat was a matter of survival and every home kept a fire going in daytime winter. Some homes had a cook stove and a fireplace, but many like ours, had a cook stove and a wood heater. Whatever the case, smoke boiled from every house in the country until bedtime.

Nobody kept a fire all night, because nobody wanted to get out of a warm bed at midnight to keep a fire going when nobody was awake to stay warm by it. The biggest reason was all the extra wood it would take. Nobody wanted to cut wood around the clock to keep a fire going around the clock, while everybody was asleep in a good warm bed.

Pa was the fireman and on cold winter mornings, we came out of bed and shivered until he got the heater fired up. "Ain't nobody never gonna' be cold in this house as long as the wood holds out." We kept a steaming bucket of water on top to put moisture into the dry air. At bedtime, we dived into icy beds again and shivered again until we got warm.

With the coming of October, we headed for the woods to cut winter firewood. Everybody knew how to use a crosscut saw and swing an axe and by wintertime, everybody had a huge stack of wood. Anyone too old or sick to cut their own found out how good their neighbors were and nobody did without firewood.

When Pa cut a tree, he first figured out which way it would fall and we cleared out a path in the other direction. "If it falls the wrong way, boy, you be ready to run." As it began falling, we ran: just in case it split and kicked backwards. (They always fell the right way.)

We trimmed off the limbs, "snaked" it home with the horse and sawed it into stove wood. Apparently I made it harder on Pa because he told me, "Boy, I ain't gonna' tell you many more times to ease up on that saw when I pull it my way, so I don't have to pull you and the saw too."

The hardest job known to mankind was sawing wood with a dull crosscut saw; you could pull it back and forth all day and not much happened. Dead trees dulled the saw teeth faster than green trees, but to Pa's credit, he kept the saw teeth sharp. We started fires with dry (dead) wood and when they were burning well, we switched to greener wood, which burned longer.

Staying warm in winter was hard work, but with the heater jumping off the floor on cold winter days, nobody backed away. Coming in from a cold backwoods mission and thawing my frozen feet by the red-hot heater made all the woodcutting worthwhile.

The low-in-the-sky winter sun shined directly into a south facing kitchen window: giving enough heat to sit there and read and be comfortable. The oil lamp chimney gave enough heat to warm cold hands while reading on cold winter nights.

One of our neighbors didn't cut his firewood; he stayed warm by feeding a long dry pole into the open firebox door on his cook stove. He kept the pole propped level with a chair and as it burned, he pushed it farther into the stove. If we'd tried that at our house, the pole would've been propped on the kitchen table. No way would that work, because nothing got in Pa's way at meal times, or any other time, for that matter.

Keeping the barn flues, cook stove, heater and wash pot burning took a bunch of trees. When money was scarce, Pa sometimes sold some oak, poplar and pines for timber, but we burned far more than we sold. One local family burned every tree on their small farm, but thanks to caring neighbors, they too had firewood for winter.

After all the trees were cut from an area, new sprouts came up at the stumps and it was called a "sprout patch." Our main tobacco field was a sprout patch until we dug out the roots, stumps and rocks: using dynamite, the horse, the mattock and our hands. It was hard work but when finished, we had a brand new field called a "new ground."

With the exception of bottomland, new grounds were the best land on any farm and everybody tended them year after year until they were completely worn out. Then they cleared off another new ground and continued right along.

I remember two sprout patches that never became new grounds: one on a hillside at Grandpa's and the other at Jim Smith's place on Lambsburg Road. Both Grandpa and Jim had cleared many new grounds, but they were getting older and didn't need any more new fields. "Can't take care a' what I got now."

On another day in a later year, heavy snow was again falling at daylight, as Mama cooked breakfast. The smells of homemade sausage, buckwheat pancakes and white-sop gravy filled the house and just as in earlier years, Pa said, "Git outta' that bed, boys, she's a' snowin' heavy out yonder." Once again, he tuned the radio to a weather forecast from WJJD, Chicago and told us, "It's cold as Hell out there in Chicago."

There could be no better time than watching snow fall from the sky while eating a great breakfast. The slingshots of younger years were long-gone, but with .22 rifle, a box of bullets and a big white world to track rabbits in, what else could anybody need? Everything I needed and wanted was waiting just outside the door.

Several weeks of freezing winter weather tended to darken people's souls and when shut inside for days on end, they became depressed. Everything readable had been read twice or three times, all the old tales had been told and re-told and everybody came down with cabin fever, including us kids.

As the days dragged on, daydreams turned to spring, warm sunny days and white fluffy clouds. Somewhere down south, spring was about to wake up and head north. It was a slow-mover, but faith and the old folks promised we'd soon have green mountains to climb again, rivers to run, catfish to catch and long summer days to scout the backwoods. We'd come out of long-handled underwear, go barefooted and nekkid and never be cold again.

Best of all, we'd have gardens again, with good stuff to eat growing everywhere. No longer would we live on pinto beans, stale fatback, last year's apples and last year's canned stuff.

We knew, as did everybody else, our very lives depended on the food we coaxed from the Earth in some form or another. Without a little sunshine and rain, there'd be no food or people to eat it and food was one of the things I liked best: maybe even better than fishing, hunting, scouting and reading books.

Unending faith told us Mother Nature would once again bring rain and sunshine, just like she always did. On cold winter days, we sat by the heater and daydreamed big-time: spring would come early, the rains would come at the right time and we'd grow more stuff than we'd know what to do with. Without even going out of the house, we grew the best gardens the world had ever known. Our watermelons would be as big as a washtub and our cornstalks would reach the sky. We'd have so much good stuff to eat, we'd have to hire help to eat it all and we might need to build a bigger sled to haul it on.

Good crops depended on so many things: moon signs, faith, experience, the right temperatures, good rains, good luck and good hard work. (If there was any such a thing.) Our ancestors had it down to a science, "Don't plant too early, too late, too little or too much. Plant early stuff as soon as the ground can be worked and plant late stuff after the last frost." When a late frost came, there was only one option: do it all over again and according to Grandma, it was always Grandpa's fault, because he read the signs wrong.

As the almanac told it, "Plant stuff that grows above the ground, like beans corn, and tomatoes in the light of the moon. Plant stuff that grows below the ground, like potatoes and peanuts, in the dark of the moon." As always, there was only one best time to plant and it had better be done right. With Blum's Almanac, faith, moon signs, pure blind luck and Grandma, failure was not even an option; we had it made in the shade.

January Mail

    Like a gift from the Gods, seed catalogues came in the January mail, a breath of fresh air in the dead of winter. They became our bibles and we wore them dog-eared planning new crops and gardens. On cold snowy days, we "sot by the far," read and re-read them from cover to cover and daydreamed about all the good stuff we'd grow next summer.

    Seeds saved from last year were worth their weight in gold, but the great catalogue pictures promised even bigger and better things. Just buy a few packs of special seeds and we'd grow watermelons, tomatoes and cucumbers like nobody had ever seen before. We'd just stick some seeds in the ground and get out of the way, while Mother Nature worked her magic.

    Having very little money, we could never buy all the seeds we wanted, so we chose carefully. When the order came in the mail, the pictures on the seed packets looked even better than the catalogue pictures and promised even bigger and better stuff than we'd already planned.

    As the days grew longer, a brighter sun came up every morning and some warm days in February gave us a temporary break from the cold and melted mental icicles from frozen minds. We knew it was way too early for spring, but it was a sign of things to come and promised a spring that was already on its way north from somewhere down in Georgia.

    As the March winds howled outside, we sat by the wood heater, read Blum's Almanac and counted our blessings. With new seeds on hand, a mess of creecies cooking on the stove and spring coming from just over the hill, what else could anybody need? We'd almost made it through another winter and beyond a doubt, it would be the best year anybody "ever seen." `

Chapter 14

Spring

As the days grew longer, the dreams of winter became the dreams of summer: long barefoot days in the warm sunshine, the green woods and fields full of good things to eat; Stewart's Creek running deep, muddy and full of catfish. From somewhere down in Georgia, summer was coming and it would be a good one, if it would only speed it up a little.

With Old Man Winter still throwing wind snow from Bobbitt Holler', we knew it was much too early for spring. Even worse, the groundhog saw his shadow in early February, which meant six more weeks of bad weather. To make matters worse, the calendar showed spring beginning March twenty-first, which made it almost seven weeks.

"Easter" flowers (daffodils)

As February came on, green "Easter Flowers" (daffodils) came up in the flowerbed again and melting snow banks began long downhill journeys to the Atlantic Ocean. It had been a long cold winter, but finally, at long last, we knew for sure, spring was coming.

Creecies

As the snow melted, we headed for last year's cornfields to gather the first mess of creecies. They were small flat-on-the-ground green plants that grew slowly all winter and began growing faster along about February. When eaten with the same old everyday pinto beans, corn bread and fatback, that first mess of creecies almost single-handedly cured winter.

Cold weather no longer ruled our lives and it was almost fun to break a sweat again while we sawed wood. The whole world turned to mud and according to Mama, we tracked every bit of it into the house. "You all git' out yonder and clean them feet off before you come in here. I could plant a cornfield on that rug." (Who had time to worry about mud and who could help it if it followed them home? With so many rules and regulations to keep up with, anybody might as well be in jail.)

The sun came up earlier each day, bringing more daylight and more changes. The muddy roads dried out and cars could once again make it through the Big Mud Hole without getting stuck. I could once again ride my bicycle all the way through it without wrecking and drowning in muddy water.

One cold February day, Warren, our dog and I were playing in a south-facing broom-straw field. (Even the dog knew the south side was the warmest side on cold sunny days.) Pa and Mama were back home by the wood heater discussing each other's lousy ancestors, a problem they worked on for more than fifty years.

Grandpa and Grandma were at home by their fireplace down in the valley, "Snuffing ashes" as Grandpa said it, while Grandma discussed Grandpa's sorry ancestors. If Grandma had any ancestors, good or bad, I never heard Grandpa tell her about them. He just listened patiently, but sometimes escaped to the tack room at the horse barn.

While playing in the broom straw, we heard something that sounded like foxhounds running in the sky. From high overhead, "wild geese" (Canada Geese) come honking from the south in a V formation: on the way north for the summer. They brought a message of hope for winter-logged minds, "Spring is just back there where we came from and it's headed this way. Come along with us and help spread the word." How I wished, but since it could never happen, I just stood there spellbound as they flew out of sight toward Hillsville.

According to the old timers, "When you see them wild geese flyin' north, boy, you'll know spring ain't far behind." There'd never really been much doubt, but we now knew for sure: we'd seen the worst of the "worst winter I ever seen."

Some 40 years later, I was repairing Dolly Marshall's satellite system (across the valley from our old home place) when Canada geese come honking up over the trees in a v formation. It was sight I hadn't seen since that long-ago February day and I just stood there spellbound. They circled around overhead and flew back down toward Watershed Lake, as cold chills crawled all up and down my back.

In the old days, we only saw wild geese when they migrated in spring and fall and they flew very high in the sky. (By the 1980s, most no longer migrated, but stayed in our area all year. As of today, they can be seen most anytime, flying low overhead in V-formations; honking their way to somebody's cornfield.)

The rooster crowed each morning at the crack of dawn, telling the sun to get out of bed; it would never have made it without his help. Birds sang everywhere: telling the world it was spring again. Honeybees swarmed on yellow dandelion blooms and before very long, dandelion seeds floated in the air like small white parachutes, headed for far places to make new dandelions next year. As the sap rose again, red maple sprouts became even redder and new buds swelled on every bush and tree.

After freezing to death all winter, warm weather was just like getting out of jail. Mother Earth came alive and everything smelled fresh and new. A warm breeze from the east brought on a brand new season and there was no longer any doubt in anybody's mind: summer was coming from just over the South Forty and everybody and everything in the whole country was long past ready, especially me.

"Sarvice" (service) blooms

"Sarvice" (Service) trees bloomed white again in February's bare woods and I tried to remember where, when the berries ripened in mid-summer. Maple trees bloomed red down the valley and in almost no time, dogwood and redbud blooms covered the hillsides at Oscar Marshall's bottoms. All other trees bloomed in their own time, as apple, peach, pear, plum and cherry trees followed soon after.

Tobacco plant bed, with cover supports

The blooming service trees told us it was time to clear off a new tobacco plant bed. We grubbed roots and rocks, burned brush, plowed and smoothed the bed, framed it with poles and shoveled dirt around them to keep them in place. When the signs were right, we fertilized the ground and sowed tobacco seeds saved from last year's plants.

We raided Grandpa's sprout patch for dozens of pencil-sized twigs about two feet long and pushed both ends of the twigs into the ground to make bows that held the plant bed cover a few inches off the ground. The white covers helped keep out the cold and could be seen on every farm in early spring. Some larger farms had two or more beds, but we only had one. (While priming tobacco in the hot summer sun, I wished we'd had none.)

In almost no time, the tobacco seeds came up, even in the ice, snow and freezing rain. On warm sunny days, we rolled the covers back to give the plants air and sunshine. If the weather turned cold again, we re-covered the bed and if it failed to rain, we watered the beds with a barrel of rainwater hauled on the sourwood sled. We never had a plant-bed failure.

Sourwood trees bloomed in mid-June: long after dogwoods and other trees. A heavy sourwood bloom meant a heavy crop of sourwood honey, which Mama used to make the cookies that kept the world turning when she ran out of sugar. Anytime we found a bee tree full of sourwood honey, we'd already had a good year.

Built-in instincts drove everything in Mother Nature to prepare for next year. Poplar trees, blackberry briars and grass led the re-greening of the Earth and new grass out-grew everything under the sun except weeds in the garden. Once *they* got a taste of fertilizer, they grew twice as fast as anything else, "Boys, that garden stuff out there's gonna' be your supper next winter and if you want anything to eat then, you better make them weeds fly." (I became a master weed-puller and made "them weeds fly.")

There was new life in every direction and somewhere, somehow, some way, the cow found a new calf in a hollow log and neighbors gave us a new puppy. Baby rabbits ran everywhere, but running as fast as I could, I never caught one.

There were two birds in every bush: all singing their springtime songs. Bluebirds sat on old fence posts, watched the sky and searched for a place to nest. Robins came home from the winter woods and proudly showed off their red breasts. They hopped all over the back yard and somehow, pulled fish worms from the ground where I could see no worms.

The rooster crowed at first light to welcome the new day. He was a proud bird, who strutted around the yard all day looking important, while the hens did all the work: minding the little ones and laying eggs. To his credit, he flogged anything that bothered his flock, including me: especially me.

Each year, Grandpa went into the woods and gathered an assortment of green-all-year herbs to make his "herb bitters: a "spring tonic to cure winter-thickened blood." He believed that anything that could survive winter temperatures had special healing properties. He crushed the leaves in a fruit jar of water and kept the frightening concoction cold in the springhouse.

I think it did the job, because he was never sick and could drink the stuff straight from the jar without frowning. He said, "Boy, that's good stuff." As the name "bitters" implies, it tasted awful and after only one taste, I knew my blood was already thin enough.

Pa made his own blood thinner far in the backwoods and his was more powerful than Grandpa's, because he was a happy man when he drank a few slugs. He too drank it straight from the jar and said, "Boy, that's good stuff. To me, it tasted even worse than Grandpa's bitters. I think faulty tasters ran in our family.

When oak trees bloomed, yellow pollen rings gathered around the outer edges of mud puddles and a few days later, pine pollen made white rings in the same puddles. When the sun was low in the evening sky, you could see pollen drifting in the air. It caused some people to sniffle, sneeze and wheeze, but it never bothered me.

Poplar trees leafed out first in spring: beginning as a light green tinge in the hillsides and followed soon after by maples and oaks. In almost no time, all the leaves on all the trees were grown and dark green. "Whatever the weather, boys, them leaves'll be full-grown by the tenth of May."

Our foothills greened-up first, followed soon after by the mountainsides. As the days went by, the green climbed higher and higher toward Galax and Hillsville and in almost no time, the whole mountain was dark green, instead of the deep blue it had been all winter.

Every spring, Pa and I went through the same routine when the leaves began growing. I said to him, "The trees sure are turning green in a hurry." He said, "Fastest I ever seen." He didn't realize we said the same thing every year and I finally became ashamed and quit saying it. The next spring, I almost had to bite my tongue to keep from telling him how fast the woods were turning green.

(In 2007, a late freeze came on Easter weekend that killed all the new leaves, including those on the mountain. The whole country turned brown, then all the leaves fell off, then, before very long, new leaves grew again. I'd never seen that happen before.)

As spring came on, we squished barefoot in mud puddles and watched frog eggs turn into tadpoles. "You all stay outta' them mud holes, or you gonna' git' toe itch, warts and no telling what all splashing around in there. You might even turn web-footed like a duck and you gonna' look funny a flappin' and a quackin'."

When the cow found the new calf, we had milk to drink again and real white-sop gravy instead of water gravy. When the smell of pancakes, gravy and fried sausage filled the house, nobody had to drag me out of bed. The biggest problem was avoiding a wreck with a speeding brother on the way to the table. When the cow went dry again, we had no more milk unless Grandpa and Grandma had some to share.

After a hen sat on her eggs for a few days, we had baby widdies running all over the place. The puppy chased the widdies, the mama hen chased the puppy, we chased her, the rooster chased us and we had ourselves a convoy. Robins nested in the grapevines and bluebirds built in a hollow fence post. Anybody who dared go near either got dive-bombed. When a hawk raided a crow's nest beside the Graveyard Road, a dozen other crows flew in and chased it away.

Pa was always at war with something: stray horses, mules, cows, dogs or a sneaky neighbor. Hawks were high on his list and to his way of thinking, there was only one kind: they were all "chicken hawks" and needed "their hides filled with lead." He kept an eye on the sky and when one dive-bombed our baby chicks, he seldom missed. Both chicken hawks and suck-egg dogs lived a hard life on our hill.

Planning a new season was serious business, because mistakes could mean total disaster next winter. There was only one best time to plant and "you better git'er' right the first time or you're wastin' time and money." With knowledge passed down by generations of ancestors and our own hard-earned lessons, we planned every detail for the coming year. Grandpa and Grandma knew what to plant; Blum's Almanac told us when to plant and the seed catalogues told us where and how to plant. Throw in a little luck and no way under the sun could we fail.

We had no horse, plows, or wagon in the early years and without my grandparent's help, our home would've been the Poor House in Dobson. We swapped work with them, borrowed their horse and plows to "turn" our land," cultivate our corn and tobacco crops and at harvest time, we hauled our corn, fodder and tops back home on their wagon. We also cured our tobacco in their barns.

We never owned a wagon, but when Pa bought a horse, we built our own sourwood sled and began climbing out of the deep hole we started in. (It was our only means of transportation until he bought a used 1931 A-Model in 1948.)

Beginning with the ridge fields, which dried out first, Pa and Grandpa plowed the land in early spring. All day long they ploughed and kept an eye on the sky for signs of coming weather. I wondered how they could tell anything by looking up at a clear blue sky, when all I could see was a bird or an airplane. They "rough-ploughed" with a one-horse hillside turning plow and when the sun finally went down behind the mountain, they limped back home, rested all night and come next morning, they did it all over again.

Pa made no plowing mistakes, but when the commands got mixed up, it was always a horse problem. When it strayed out of bounds, he told it, "You already know which way to go, you hellion and if I had a rock, I'd straighten you out." (He sometimes used stronger language that the horse understood well.)

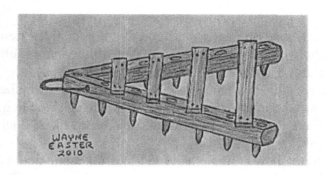

The "harr"

After "turning the land", they broke-up the dirt clods with Grandpa's homemade wooden harrow. (We called it a "harr".) It was made of two logs fastened in a V-shape, with wooden teeth and the horse pulled it back and forth across the fresh-plowed fields until the land was smooth. When a tooth hit a rock and broke, they replaced it. (In later years, Pa built our own harrow with metal teeth (railroad spikes) that didn't break.)

After "harring the land to death," they "layed-off" the rows, as the horse pulled the lay-off plow back and forth across the fields. Saying "gee" made the horse go right and saying "Haa," made it go left: sometimes. When that didn't work, yanking on the right or left plow line did the trick for Pa. "Gotta' git them rows straight, boy, or stuff ain't gonna' grow right."

The empty Kasco Feed and Seed Store building on Market Street (2009)

With the coming of spring, Pa and Grandpa headed for Kasco's Feed and Seed Store on Market Street in Mt Airy to buy seeds and fertilizer, with a promise to "pay this fall." As it was with mountain people, their handshake was their bond and they paid their debts, always.

There was nothing under the sun like a little faith, something every farmer was loaded with. Spring would come early, the rains would come at the right time and it would be a year like no other. "Them corn ears'll hang so high, we'll have to climb a ladder to pick 'em and them punkins' and melons'll be so big we'll have to be saw 'em up with a crosscut saw and haul 'em home one slice at a time. We might even have to hire help to eat it all."

We followed the old ways at planting time, as well as most other times for that matter, "Plant 'em deep in dry weather and not so deep in wet weather and don't put no clods on top of the seeds. Plant by the signs or you're wastin' your time, let alone all that money."

We always (to hear us tell it) followed the moon signs and did it just like we did it last year, which was the way it was supposed to be done. When we couldn't remember how that was, we "planted 'er by guess, by crackity." Sometimes, Heaven forbid, we planted when the signs were wrong, especially when rain was coming. I already knew stuff "growed good" if it rained and didn't grow good if it didn't. Whatever the weather, weeds headed for the sky, always, every time, so what else was there to know?

We planted peas, beets and onion sets as soon as the ground dried out enough to work. Irish potatoes "went in" after the full moon in March: "half a tater to a hill with the eyes up and don't put 'em on the fertilize and don't put no clods on top of the tater." We planted last year's sweet potatoes in a bed to make plants to be "sot out in the middle of May when the ground warms up real good."

We sowed last-year's tomato seeds in a worn-out dishpan of dirt. When they began growing, Mama placed them outside during the day, unless the weather was too cold; then she brought them inside out of danger. We set tomato plants by the dozens the last week in April and sometimes that was too early. When a late freeze wiped out everything in sight, we had no choice but to do it all over again.

We planted half-runner beans "not too deep" on Good Friday, unless it came too early. We planted corn fields when white oak leaves became the size of a squirrel's ear: "two grains to a hill and don't put 'em on the fertilize."

Cornfield peas, okra, watermelons, pepper, sweet potatoes, peanuts and cantaloupes, "went in" after the ground warmed up in May. The all-time best time to plant watermelon and cantaloupe seeds was the first day of May, "before sun-up in your shirt tail."

Even the best-laid plans failed when late freezes came and there was no option, but to do it all over again. As Grandma told Grandpa, "See? I told you the almanac said it was too early, but you wouldn't listen, you old fool." Bean, squash, tomato, watermelon, and cucumber vines couldn't survive a hard freeze, but cabbage and garden peas hung on and when Irish potato vines froze out, they always came back.

Garden in early spring (1960s)

We followed Blum's Almanac, the calendar, moon signs, Mother Nature, our own memory and advice from Grandma. When we couldn't remember how we did it last year, we did it the way we thought it should be done. Even with late frosts, hail, drought, wind, marauding animals and sneaky neighbors, it all worked out in the end. Grandpa knew it would work all along, "Them rains'll come when they git ready, boy." They always came, sometimes just in the nick of time.

The garden in winter: at the home place on Banjo Lane (1970s)

When the fence wire rusted away at the first garden, we started a new one beside the barn: with no fence. As Pa told it, "Every varmint in the whole damn country heads straight for my garden. The next milk cow I see in there ain't coming out alive and we gonna' be eatin' steak." That was a plan I could live with, because we ate very little steak on our hill.

We planted cornfields, tobacco fields and any other kind of field Pa could find; anytime he found one made of dirt, we planted something in it. When the fields were too wet to plow, normal people went fishing on Stewart's Creek. The only problem: there was no "normal" at our house; we headed to the South Forty to saw flue wood for the tobacco barns. Flue wood needed to be "about dry" by curing time and if not cut early and in the right moon sign, it wouldn't burn right. (There were perfectly logical reasons for doing everything we did and how we did it.)

When heating season ended, we stored the wood heater in the barn. By then, winter was just a bad dream that had already gone back over the mountain to wherever it came from: somewhere beyond Hillsville. The world began again at the beginning and all was new once more, after "the hardest winter I ever seen."

All winter long we were told, "You come back in here and git you a coat on. You gonna' freeze to death out yonder." With the coming of spring, we heard a different tune, "What hog pen you all been wallering in? You git back out yonder and clean the mud offa' them feet before you come in here and don't slam that door when you go out, neither." (What good was a floor if you couldn't walk on it and who in blankety-blank could remember all that stuff?)

As spring came on, we came out of long handled underwear, shirts and shoes and turned dark brown in the warm sunshine. Wintertime feet were tender and white early on, but after a few days of running wide-open through rock piles and briar patches, it was no longer a problem.

All of our spring days were full, but as time passed, they got fuller. The longer days brought a longer list of things that had to be done, right now, this very minute. We plowed, planted, hoed, pulled weeds and fought flea bugs and cut worms. Anything that didn't look right or died, got re-sowed, re-planted or re-set.

The first plantings always did best but when something died, or didn't look right, we replaced it anyway. We hauled fertilizer to the fields on the sourwood sled, "hand-strowed" it in rows for tobacco plants, covered it up with the double shovel plow and set tobacco plants when the signs got right.

After a "tater growin' frog chokin' rain," we filled bushel baskets with tobacco plants from the plant bed and set them with wooden pegs. (Small sticks used to make holes in the ground.) It was all-day backbreaking work and we punched a million holes in the ground. It was even harder than priming the first leaves off the bottom of tobacco plants. By the end of pegging day, I was almost permanently shaped like the letter "A" and could hardly stand upright.

When the ground was dry, instead of pegging, we hauled a rain barrel of water to the field and set tobacco plants with a baccer' setter. It was a metal contraption with a water reservoir inside and a set of jaws on the bottom. Pa carried it from hill to hill and chunked it down into the row where a tobacco plant was to be set. When someone dropped a tobacco plant down inside the setter, Pa pulled a lever under the handle that opened the jaws on the bottom and the watering was automatic as long as water was kept in the reservoir. When he lifted the setter out of the ground, the newly watered plant remained in the dirt. Releasing the lever closed the jaws and the setter was ready for another plant.

'Baccer setter

Other than cutworms, young tobacco plants had few enemies, but when corn plants came up, crows were just waiting to pull them out of the ground and eat the grain of seed corn. Pa then shot one and hung it on a string from a tall pole to scare other crows away.

If that didn't work, he went to Plan B and set a steel trap on top of the pole. That worked best of all and saved a hard-earned shotgun shell. When a crow landed in the trap, it made so much noise every other crow in the country flew in to see what was wrong. Then they all made so much noise, everybody in the country knew Pa had caught another crow.

As spring came on, every growing plant headed for the sky and needed plowing and hoeing "right now, right this very minute." Hot weather began playing for keeps and weeds grew faster than "master weed-puller me" could pull them. I doubt if an army could've done everything we needed to do. There was no way we could be everywhere at the same time and we'd never have any playtime again. It was beginning to look like a long hot summer.

Summertime

Chapter 15

Summer

By late winter, anybody who didn't like pinto beans, fatback, and corn bread was in big time trouble. That's when thoughts turned to summer and a world full of good things to eat. The only problem, summer was still asleep somewhere down in Georgia and our only saving grace was the creecies we gathered in last year's cornfields. By the end of March, they were knee high, had bright yellow blooms and were no longer edible.

That was no longer a problem, because dandelion greens, lettuce and plantain were coming on strong. In mid-spring, we gathered the first apples of the year from an Early Transparent tree at the Hiatt House. When nobody lived there, it was finders-keepers and whoever got there first got the apples. (We lived close by and were almost always first in line.)

Irish taters'

As Irish potatoes grew, the ground cracked under the vines: showing us where to "gravel" (scratch out) the first new potatoes. They were better then than at any other time and we ate them unpeeled. For someone who was hungry twenty-four hours a day, potatoes were good anytime, regardless of how, where or *if* they were cooked. They were especially good roasted in tobacco barn flues.

Mama made pickles from poke stalks, cucumbers and watermelon rinds and made jams and jellies from gooseberries, blackberries, dewberries, apples, peaches, grapes, and plums. She canned tomatoes, beans, sausage, peas and anything else she could find. Nothing was safe on our hill and anything that we didn't can, dry, jelly or preserve, we ate.

Everybody bragged about "them good green beans." but to me, they were barely o k when eaten with new potatoes, corn bread and milk and I only ate the cussed things because of what might happen if I didn't. "If you don't like what we got to eat, boy, you go out yonder in the yard and graze." I ate the beans.

Green beans reached a low point with my first Army meal. The cooks dipped them in hot water, once, maybe and I said to myself, "Surely to God they don't expect me to eat raw green beans." (They didn't care how Mama did it back home; they did it like they did it "up north" and ate them raw.) As time passed, I got older and green beans got better.

'Maters

By the end of June, the race was on to have the firstest, finest, bestest, biggest, reddest, ripest 'mater the world had ever seen, which gave the lucky winner bragging rights for a whole year. Our neighbor once bought two huge ripe tomatoes at the store to show Pa how early his were. Pa was not impressed. We grew them by the bushels and Mama canned them by the bushels. "Gotta' can 'em while we got em' cause they may not be none next year."

Cornbread kept the wolf from more doors than all other foods combined. In very lean times, cornbread and milk were the only foods at meal times and in some drastic cases, water replaced the milk. We ate corn in the roasneer (roasting ear) stage: boiled on the cob, or cut off, cooked and served with butter. It was a feast when roasted in the oven and barn flues and I sometimes ate it raw, straight off the stalk. It was at its very best when roasted over a campfire on a Stewart's Creek sandbar.

While running important backwoods missions, experienced scouts and hunters (such as myself) kept sharp eye out for food. Thanks to the un-knowing generosity of neighbors, their summer cornfields sometimes became dinner. I felt a little guilty eating other people's corn without asking, but surely they wouldn't wish starvation on a good guy like me.

The world was a land of plenty in good old summer: gooseberries grew beside the garden fence, watermelons and mush melons cooled in the spring box and bellyaches grew on green apple trees. A wormy apple wasn't even a small problem; I just whittled the worm out with my trusty Barlow and kept right on eating.

Green "oap balls" (oak balls) grew on Spanish oak leaves, with a small worm in the white cotton ball center. Like the squirrels, I only ate the green outside shell and threw the rest away. Like the Indians, I tried eating acorns, but they were much too bitter.

Blackberries, dewberries, and wild strawberries grew in old fields and huckleberries and chinquapins grew in the sprout patch. Wild red plums and black raspberries grew along the roadsides and sarvice berries grew beside the cornfields.

There were horny heads and catfish in Stewart's Creek and fox grapes and hazel nuts on the branch banks: to say nothing of hickory nuts in the backwoods, ground cherries and wild apricots in late summer cornfields. No matter where you looked in the middle of summer, something was growing and almost all of it was good.

I found may apples, rabbit apples, honeysuckle apples and other great looking stuff, but didn't always know what was safe to eat. "You eat some a' that stuff out there, boy, you gonna' see boogers you ain't never seen before."

Some of our neighbors ate wild mushrooms and they acted a little funny. We were told, "You boys ain't got much sense no how and if you eat some a' them mushrooms, you gonna' act like them idiots over yonder and you ain't gonna' have none a'tall." (Judging by Pa and Mama's actions, I wondered if they sneaked around and ate wild mushrooms.)

Mama made part of our clothes from the white cloth flour sacks she dyed brown with walnut hulls. She later used a commercial dye called Rit to get different colors. Without the flour sacks, we'd have been "runnin' around here nekkid," as she said it. (In the good old summer time, we almost did.)

Growing boys were forever at starvation's door and anyone who fumbled getting to the table at mealtimes could get run over by a freight train. There was only one call to "come and get it" and we knew where our place was and how to get there. Pa's place was at the head of the table and "they ain't nobody brave enough to set in my cheer."

We said no blessings, but Mama tried to teach us some basic table manners. "Don't play in your food, don't eat with your fingers, don't talk with your mouth full and don't drip gravy on them clean school clothes." She gave us one bit of advice I never learned how to do, "Shut your mouth and eat." I tried hard and almost got double lockjaw.

Mama was a great cook and always fixed our meals, even when she felt poorly or was tired from working in the fields all day. When company came, she cooked extra special meals: like two fried chickens, two pans of biscuits, gravy, pies and enough food to feed an army. Nobody left our house hungry, ever.

Uncle Manuel, who lived in Oregon, once paid us a visit and Mama cooked a huge corn shucking dinner. While we were eating, he said, "Pass the fruit, please." My parent's oldest son said very seriously, "That ain't fruit! Them's apples!" Everybody there hee-hawed their heads off, while I tried to figure out what was so funny.

Pa favorite times were meal times, three times a day and what he liked best was what we had the most of: pinto beans cooked with fatback, corn bread and milk. Mama put food on his plate, "broke" his bread and waited on him hand and foot. When the meal was through, so was Pa, because he didn't wash dishes, clothes or clean house; he already had all he could do running the farm and shooting the shotgun.

New yellow "widdies" that didn't get caught by a hawk, weasel or a stray dog, grew up and became laying hens or got fried. Ours ran free in the daytime and when we needed one to eat, we had to chase it down. The whole family and the dog got into the act and chickens squawked all over our hill. The one we were chasing usually ran under the granary, which was low on the ground where we couldn't go. A long fishing pole soon put it on the road again and the chase was on again. We never failed.

When we finally caught it, Pa chopped its head off with the axe or Mama held it by the neck and whirled it around and around to break its neck. Then she scalded it in boiling water in the washtub to loosen the feathers, plucked them off, cleaned it out, cut it up and fried it up. Then came the best part: we ate it up.

It was said Primitive Baptist preachers loved fried chicken too and that's what Grandma fixed when they spent the night. She also let him sleep in the feather bed (the company bed) and Grandpa let him check out his homemade wine. No wonder preachers preached.

Pa caught mud turtles by baiting fishhooks with dough balls tied to the jugs he left floating in the creek and local fishponds. When he caught one, he cut its head off with the axe, cut the shell off with his knife, Mama parboiled, salted, peppered it, rolled the pieces in flour and fried them like chicken and according to Pa, "It was better'n chicken."

When a turtle's head was chopped off, it fell to the ground with its mouth opened wide. When we placed a stick in the mouth, it snapped shut and stayed that way. "If that thing bites down on a toe, boys, it won't turn loose 'til it thunders and you might have a long wait, because it don't thunder much around here this time of the year." (When I even thought about a turtle's head, my bare toes hid way up behind my knees.)

Pa and I made a seine from fertilizer sacks and headed for the Abe Hole. Just thinking about all the catfish we were about to seine out of Stewart's Creek put my imagination into the clouds. I wondered if we should bring the horse and sled along to haul them home. We'd be cleaning fish all night long by lantern light and talk about eating fried fish, we might even have to stand in the branch: the only known cure for getting foundered.

To avoid climbing through a tangled laurel bluff, we waded downstream to a sandbar on the other side of the creek, because it was the easiest place to get in the water. Pa told me, "Be quiet and keep the seine on the bottom of the creek and move fast as you can." The seine was hard to pull in the deep water as he waded and I floated around all over the place. I learned right away: it's hard to be quiet and move fast when your feet keep coming up off the bottom and you're about to drown: especially when you can't swim.

Most of the fish got away as I thrashed around and the few we caught probably died of fright from all my floundering. At least we cooled off in the creek and finally caught a "mess." It was my first and only seining trip and probably Pa's last.

On another too-hot-to-plow day, we headed for the same hole with dynamite. I figured we'd now get all them fish that got away before and without all that floundering and drowning and seining. Once again, we avoided the bluff and waded down to the same sandbar, because Pa said that was the best place to catch the fish as they floated by after we dynamited them.

He put a fuse and cap in a piece of dynamite, tied it to a fist-sized rock, lit the fuse and threw it in the fishing hole. It sank immediately, but the dynamite came loose from the rock, floated back to the top of the water and exploded.

Under water, it would've made a deep "whump" sound, but on top, it rattled half the county and scared me half to death. We blazed a brand new trail through the same laurel thicket we'd avoided getting there (where no man had been before) and we never looked back. We never knew if we got any fish and when neighbors asked about a loud explosion, we hadn't heard nothin'. I figured out all by myself that people could starve to death by fishing with fertilizer sack seines and dynamite.

Grandpa's bee gums were under one section of his grapevines: exactly where the biggest and best grapes grew. Most likely, they were twice as big and twice as good as ordinary grapes, but I never found out. Like hornets and yellow jackets, honeybees had stingers and I stayed far away. I figured he put the bee gums there to be sure of having enough grapes to make wine and jelly.

One of his gums swarmed one summer day and the air was full of flying buzzing bees that acted as mad as hornets. Again, I watched from far away as Grandpa beat on a pot lid until they settled into an empty log gum. I wouldn't have waded into that many bees for all the honey in the world, but when he got stung, he just slapped the bee off and continued right along. It was said bee stings would keep arthritis under control, but after a few good stings in certain places, I figured arthritis might be the better bargain.

Sourwood was the best honey of all and when the trees bloomed, we slapped bunches of the blooms against our hands, which caused a small amount of honey to come out, which we licked. "Boys, you can lick them sourwoods but don't you go lickin' none of them ivy blooms. Them things'll turn you google-eyed and kill you deader'n a door nail." As my brothers said in later years, "We growed up afraid to move."

One too-hot-to-work day, Pa and I placed a pan of old honey beside the Sawmill Road, sat under a shade tree and before very long, honeybees began feeding on it. We tracked them to a hollow chestnut oak far down in Oscar Marshall's Woods. Bees were pouring in and out of a knothole high up the tree, which meant we'd found a good one. Pa whittled an "x" on the tree bark with his pocketknife, which told the world the bee tree had already been found. (I never heard of anyone cutting someone else's bee tree.)

We came back another day and Pa and Grandpa sawed the tree down with the crosscut saw, while I watched from far away. They chopped the tree trunk apart and kept the bees under control with Grandpa's bee smoker. It burned old rags that smelled awful and made so much black smoke it looked like the woods were on fire. It was easy to see why bees stayed out of the smoke; it smelled bad enough to gag a mule.

The tree was full of honey and even after sharing with the landowner; we had more than I'd ever seen. After a big breakfast of eggs, white sop gravy, home-canned sausage and hot homemade wheat bread smeared with honey, I could hoe corn like nobody's business.

Summer wasn't all honey and roses and by the middle of June, we were dying in the hot fields. We had no thermometer and never knew how hot it really was. Day after day, the sun boiled down and I tried to think about cool things, but it was hard to imagine snow when drowning in sweat.

Some people said they could hear corn growing just after a rain and durn tootin sure as shootin', I could see weeds grow anytime. Pa's take on the subject, "The whole place'll grow up if you just stand there with a hoe in your hand. You gotta' use it, son and you better learn the difference between a bean vine and a weed, or I'll show you where Tony hid the wedge." (I finally figured out where that was.)

Our summer home was in the fields and there we stayed from daylight to dark. When I got a little draggy, Pa reminded me of the hickory-switch dances he had taught me and I kept plugging along. As the day got hotter, the sweat poured and the more we drank, the more we sweated and there was no end in sight.

With a hundred miles of cornrows to hoe, I figured we'd never get it all done and most likely, we'd die trying and run out of water on top of that. I just hoped to live long enough to catch all the whoppers in the Abe Hole before they died of old age.

We took a break at dinnertime, but all too soon, we were right back out there in the hottest part of the day. My only chance was a thunderstorm and they were few and far between in summer. Thanks to my lucky buckeye and rabbit's foot, even the hottest days finally came to an end and it was a great relief to see the sun go down behind Fisher's Peak, after "the hottest day I ever seen."

As if things could get no worse, Dog Days came in July. They were always a hot, dry, miserable time and we tried to get most of the outside work done before and after the mid-day heat. "You'll git yourself sunstroke out there, boy, and finish cookin' what little brain you got left." Meanwhile, our dog stayed in the shade, which spoke wonders about who was smartest. I could almost hear him thinking, "Don't you wish you was me?"

Rain was needed worse during Dog Days than at any other time and one sure way to bring it was to hang a dead snake on a fence or in a bush. The only good snake was a dead one anyhow and the bigger it was, the more rain it would bring. Even a small snake would bring a light shower.

The very best way to bring rain was to find a live snake resting in a bush or tree. If not bothered, it would bring a real gulley washer *that very day*. The only problem with that; snakes in mid-summer were like fish worms, they had gone to China, never to be seen again.

When someone saw a snake, to hear them tell it, "It was the biggest I ever seen." The actual size depended on who saw it and how many times they told about it. Soon after first-sighting, a foot-long snake was six feet long and big as a 'baccer setter." As someone said it, "Big around as my leg and this long." (Shown by wide spread arms.) The way it looked, people with the longest arms saw the longest snakes.

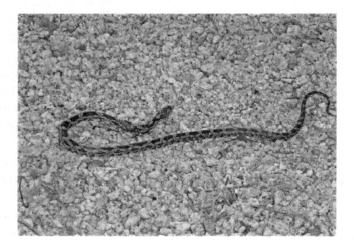

Copperhead

We learned to identify all kinds of snakes: especially copperheads. "You all stay outta' them old lumber stacks and rock piles and slab piles, 'cause that's where them varmints den up. Snakes is blind in Dog Days, but they can still bite you and watch out for them black racers 'cause they can run faster'n you can."

Pa said hoop snakes were the worst kind of all, "They take their tails in their mouths and make big hoops and come rolling downhill and they ain't no way you can out-run 'em." I was a good learner, as well as a good runner and kept an eye out for black racers. When going uphill, I kept both eyes out for any hoop snakes that might come rolling downhill.

Blacksnakes lived in our granary and ate the mice that ate the corn, but when one got inside the house, we tore it apart trying to find it. When we finally did, nobody cared whether it was poison or not; it was a goner. Some people tangled with rattlesnakes, but that was one of the few varmints we never had to deal with.

I seldom thought about snakes and that was the case when coming back from the mailbox one day. I was bouncing along barefoot and humming a new tune: fully lost in another world, when a black snake suddenly appeared right out of the blue, coiled up in the middle of the road right in front of me.

I figured to be "eat plumb up" already and jumped about three feet high. For all practical purposes, I walked on air and somehow we missed each other. I hit the ground running and looked back to see if a black racer was chasing me. I was already pouring on the coal, but if it had been, no doubt about it, I'd have dug deeper and found some more speed.

It was said big snows "wiped out all them cussed varmints," but regardless of how many we had in winter, or how deep they were, we never had a shortage of stinging, biting aggravating pests in summer. Chiggers were right on top of the list and anytime I raided a blackberry or huckleberry patch, I got "all eat up."

We tangled with snakes, hornets, yellow jackets, "waspers", bumble bees, black widders', 'skeeters, ticks, gnats, poison ivy, sheep flies, horse flies and blue-tailed scorpins': all of which were life-threatening. "You keep your eyes open out there, boys, or you'll git eat alive and you won't know nothin' about it."

Dr. Mama sometimes saved our lives with an application (the bigger the better) of red Mercurochrome or Iodine. She used Mercurochrome on ordinary hurts, but for the big hurts, she brought out the big gun: Iodine, which burned like fire. The bigger the area painted by either, the better the hurt place looked. "Boy, I got hurt bad, didn't I?"

It was a known fact that fleas would travel a mile to bite me. If I even met a stray dog in the road, I would soon be "eat alive." For that very reason, stray dogs were never my friends and when I met one anywhere, we made wide circles around each other, especially if we'd met before.

Mama gave us a tick inspection every day and often found one or two or three: usually before they'd bitten deeply. Most turned loose when we elevated their temperature with a burning match, then she brought out the big gun again and sterilized the place. "If you all quit wallerin' with the dogs and cats, you won't have no fleas and ticks.

As summer rolled along, we harvested everything in sight: when onion tops fell over, we tied them in bunches and hung them up to dry. We strung green beans (leather britches) to air-dry, canned more green beans and tomatoes in half-gallon fruit jars. We canned Indian Peaches, which for some reason were never as wormy as other types. We picked blackberries, dewberries and huckleberries, which we canned, jellied and made pies from. By fall of the year, the basement shelves were loaded beyond belief.

As always during Dog days, rain and thunder stayed beyond the mountain and the world dried completely up. A month-long drought brought Stewart's Creek down to half its normal size and my raging river became a spring branch. It was too small to fish, but that didn't matter, because fish worms had already gone to China. We also couldn't swim or wade, because of some slimy green stuff that covered the under-water rocks. "That green stuff'll eat your toes off."

As the long hot days dragged on, we kept an eye on the sky for signs of coming weather. "Did you see that circle around the moon last night? Them two stars inside says we'll have rain in two days." (I thought about doing some Indian rain dances to see if it would help.)

Pastures dried completely up and everything outside the fence looked like a feast to the animals. When Pa saw Old Bossy with her head through the fence, he threatened her with a hoe handle. "Git back in there, you heifer, or I'll break your neck." That worked just fine until he was out of sight, then she tried to push the fence down again.

I sat under an apple tree on Jim's Knob and watched dust clouds climb into the sky, as A-Models and T-Models traveled the dry dirt roads of summer. With a car's radiator boiled, people stopped at the first branch and refilled it with a bucket, tin can or a fruit jar.

The handiest place was at a spring branch that ran under the road near Walter Marshall's tobacco barn on Lambsburg Road. On the very hottest days, people often refilled themselves. It didn't matter that Walter's pasture was upstream and it also didn't matter that his cows didn't always get out of the branch to do their business. It was a known fact that water got purified as it ran over rocks and sand. Somebody said it was in the bible. Another said," Been drankin' branch water all my life and I ain't dead yet." (I drank from Stewart's Creek and kept living.)

Warm weather came on slowly in spring of the year, but once it got under way, it ran wide-open. First thing I knew, we were curing tobacco in Grandpa's tobacco barns. I stayed all night with Pa, as he cured and I roasted apples, 'taters and roasneers' in the flue fires and watched the sky.

I found the Big Dipper, the North Star and watched shooting stars streak by: almost too fast to see. Lightning bugs blinked in the dark and heat lightning flashed in the sky beyond the mountain, too far away to hear the thunder. Foxhounds bayed in the far Gardner Woods and a foxhunter blew his cow-horn toward Mailbox Hill. Katydids zizzed, hoot owls hooted from the bluff across the valley and bats chased moths around the kerosene lantern.

Late in the night, we wore out and slept in the tobacco sleds where snakes couldn't get us. I went to dreamland wrapped up in old dusty quilts that smelled of cured tobacco. Pa catnapped and kept the flue-fires burning. Me? I snoozed the whole night away.

The whole world baked, sizzled and suffered, as mid-day heat waves made the hilltops shimmer. People, animals and tree leaves looked tired and worn and fields turned to stone in the relentless heat. With the crops already "laid by," we didn't need to plow or hoe anything, which would've been impossible in the hard ground. Except for jobs that absolutely had to be done: like priming tobacco and canning food, most others were put on hold. It was almost too hot to eat inside and stayed that way into the wee hours; making it hard to go to sleep. The katydids never slept and sawed wood all night long.

Tired travelers rested in laurel shade at the Little Spring, drank cold water from a tin cup and told tall tales of other dry spells in other years. They told of wildfires in the mountain that lit up the nighttime sky and the wildfire that burned Jim's Knob in the 1930s. They told of the locust year when there was almost no rain and the summer of 1930 when it didn't rain from June until the middle of August.

That was the year all the crops died in the fields. "Them was the fields of Hell that summer, boy and nobody made seed and fertilize' money back." Bottomland cornfields that "never failed" did that year. It was the worst drought in memory and some families had very little to eat that winter.

Grandma Easter told of storm clouds that came up over the mountain that summer: with thunder, but no rain. That was the year the ever-faithful almanac failed. "When that don't work no more, boy, you ain't got much left to go on." My parents said the summer of 1932 (the year I was born) was almost as bad and nothing grew well.

We never knew how hot it was in the fields of summer, but we kept plugging along. By the grace of the Gods and Pa's hickory switches, I lived through some of "the hottest days I ever seen." There were times when I knew the world was about to dry up, blow away and take me right along with it.

Unlike me, Grandpa never lost the faith, "Them rains'll come when they get ready, boy." Pa's saying worked almost as well, "If she don't rain again someday, she's gonna' be a long dry spell." As it came to be, both were right and somehow, some way, the rains always came: sometimes just when needed worst and we survived.

Part 6

Hope

The beginning of fall

Chapter 16

Fall

Sometime in the middle of the night, when nobody was looking, summer came rolling downhill out of gear and passed everything in sight. Just a few days ago, we were still hoeing corn and tobacco and sweating our lives away in the hot fields. Now, here it was late August already and we were pulling fodder, cutting corn tops and priming tobacco. As the old folks put it, "You think time's a goin' fast now, boy, you just wait'll you git older, time'll go so fast, you gonna' wonder where your whole life went."

I hadn't forgotten those long rows of corn we hoed back in the summer, when the burning sun stood still in the sky, just like it did in the bible. Some days I thought it would never go down, but it always did, then the nights raced by and next day, we did it all over again.

Pulling fodder and cutting corn tops were easy jobs and I could dilly-dally along daydreaming and not paying attention. I never thought about fodder worms until a sting or two or three stopped the wool gathering. They were inch long, half-inch wide, mean, green little devils that lived on the corn leaves and had a sting all out of proportion to their size. Nobody had to tell me when I got stung; I knew it right away.

Just like they said would happen, a thunderstorm in mid-August brought an end to Dog Days and sent them back down south where they came from. After being gone all summer, "Virgil and Mary," as Grandpa called it, came up over the trees again: "a sure sign of fall."

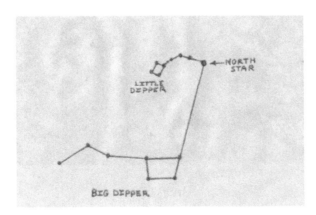

The Big and Little Dippers and the North Star. (In fall of the year.)

The Virgin Mary was an o k star, such as it was, but to my way of thinking, the North Star was the most important one in the sky. It was part of the Big and Little Dipper constellations and the whole nighttime heavens made a complete circle around it in a year's time. It was always at the same place in the sky and that would come in handy if, Heaven forbid, I ever got lost in the nighttime woods.

I'd heard some terrible crashing noises that sounded like something big as all outdoors was tearing the woods down and having no flashlight or lantern; it scared the daylights out of me. On top of that, Old Blind Topsy (who'd died years ago) was said to still be out there and "got somebody" every now and then. Nobody really believed all that stuff, but when I heard the crashing noises, I needed to be somewhere else, anywhere else, now. The last thing I needed was to get lost in the woods at night and "git got" by my worst nightmare.

I counted a million stars in the nighttime sky and tried to learn the names of some of the brightest. Blum's Almanac showed pictures of constellations with lines drawn between the stars to indicate different signs of the Zodiac. With no lines between the *real* stars, it was hard to see the bears and rams and fishes that were supposed to be there.

I saw evening stars, morning stars and now and then a shooting star streaked by: almost too fast to see. How in the world could anything go that fast? The Milky Way looked like a white paint smear across the sky, but was made up of millions, if not billions, or was it trillions of stars just like the sun. I tried, but could never sort them out, even with my telescope.

The August thunderstorm brought an end to Dog Days and evening shadows became deep, dark and long. From beyond Low Gap in the southwest, to as far as the eye could see in the northeast, the mountains continued: finally fading into the horizon somewhere in Virginia.

As nighttime temperatures dropped into the fifties, katydids quit zizzing and the silence was weird. Bed sheets felt cool once again and sleep came easier under the tin roof. Early morning spider webs covered the grass and weeds, all shining brightly with dew, but the warming sun soon dried them invisible.

As the temperatures went down, spirits went up and it felt good to breathe deep again without scorching your lungs. The thunderstorm washed all the green slime out of Stewart's Creek and lo and behold, we could wade again without dying from "green foot," or whatever the heck it was it caused. We knew hot weather would come again, but as for right now, "the hottest time I ever seen" was just a memory and a brand new fall was coming from "just over that mountain back yonder."

Breakfast

Squirrel-hunting season never ended on Stewart's Creek, but the best time was in late summer when squirrels began eating hickory nuts. They were almost as good as fried chicken and their tails made a rocket out of a bicycle when tied to its handlebars.

We sneaked in under the hickory trees in early morning and waited for them to come in to feed. Pa hunted with his shotgun and I hunted with my single-shot .22. I learned to hold my breath, aim carefully, get my mouth in the just right shape, squeeze the trigger and kill most of those I shot at. Pa never missed, because he "threw the most lead." Grandpa told of huge packs of migrating squirrels that came through the country before the chestnut trees died. All were going in the same direction, but nobody knew where they were headed or why.

Beginning in mid-August, "whipperwills" flew all over the sky in every direction: headed south for the winter. Wood chickens cackled in the Cleve Thomas Woods, hunting worms and bugs in dead trees and stumps. Before very long, we'd be in the same woods breaking ivy and pulling galax leaves: trying to make some extra money, sometimes our only money.

We sowed the salet patch, prayed for rain and Pa told us once again, "If she don't rain again some day, boys, she's gonna' be a long dry spell." The rains always came and the salet came up: became greener and greener, as everything else became browner and browner. In almost no time, we were eating turnip greens and curly-leaf mustard with our corn bread and milk. We dried apples, dug potatoes, pulled fodder, cut tops and winter firewood. We tied tobacco in Grandpa's pack-house basement and picked fox grapes: Pa made fox grape wine and Mama made fox grape jelly.

From somewhere over the mountain, winter was coming and according to the signs, the almanac and Grandpa, it would be a "mean un'. Wooly worms were black all over, crawled all over and every last one was headed south: foretelling a hard winter. The acorn crop was "heaviest I ever seen" and corn shucks were twice as thick as last year. "That cow, she growed' a brand new coat might near overnight and when them apples fell off the tree, they rolled straight downhill under the house and hid in a dark corner."

Blum's Almanac predicted a rough winter in the southeast, which was our neck of the woods and as Grandpa said it, "They'll be forty snows this winter, boy: one for every foggy morning we had in August, so you better lay in a bunch a' firewood. Them snows're comin' and they'll be plumb up to here, you wait and see. Summer's done gone south with the whipperwills' and they went early. All them signs pint' to a hard winter and you better be ready. Just thinking about all that snow makes these old bones ache fierce."

Joe Pye Weed

Joe Pye weeds bloomed purple in the late August sunshine: some so tall they leaned over into the roadways. All were covered with butterflies, but by mid-September, the purple was gone and the butterflies had moved on to other things. Goldenrods bloomed deep yellow in old fields and white milkweed blooms floated by on invisible air currents, headed on unknown journeys to unknown lands to grow new milkweeds next summer.

Green leaves, grass, and weeds looked tired and worn from the long hot summer: just like me. The raspberry vines that grew this year's berries were already dead, but the new white vines were ready and waiting for next year. Blue jays and squirrels ate white oak acorns and "fall spiders" built huge webs under the house eaves to trap insects; all preparing for winter.

We pulled fodder, cut tops and ate the wild apricots and paper-hull ground cherries that grew in late-season cornfields. Maybe, just maybe, the last tomatoes and late green beans would make it and with tobacco still to prime, it was a race between time and the first frost. We couldn't afford to lose the wrappers, (the top leaves) which were used for cigar wrappers and brought the most money. Whatever happened, with the basement full of canned stuff, potatoes, apples and pumpkins, no way would anybody go hungry on our hill.

Chinquapins once ripened in September hillsides, but as the years passed, there were fewer and fewer and just like the chestnut trees, all eventually died. They still grew "over the mountain" and we went "chinkypin huntin" along the Blue Ridge Parkway most years, usually the third week in September. One of those times, according to Ethel Smith's diary, was in September 1946. We rode in Ed Smith's pick-up and ate a picnic lunch beside the New River near Independence, Virginia. I picked so many chinquapins; I could see them that night with my eyes closed.

With the coming of September, Monarch butterflies drifted all over the sky in every direction, as they migrated south for the winter. Just like the whippoorwills, they had no apparent sense of where south was. In two different Septembers, (in the 1960s) Helen and I saw the trees on top of Jim's Knob covered with Monarch butterflies; so many the green trees were orange. Most likely, the knob was a normal rest stop for the butterflies, because, according to my journal, our daughter-in-law Pam called from their home on the knob (September 17, 2007) and said the trees were covered with orange butterflies. (They were gone next morning.)

The beginning of October brought a deep blue sky, morning chills and a promise of winter. It was said spring came north at a hundred miles a week and summer went back south at the same speed. Anybody could see spring came north a few inches a week and summer went back south at a hundred miles an hour.

Trees turned green in our area a few weeks before they did "over the mountain" and the process reversed in fall, as leaves changed color there first. Poplar trees changed color first and long after sun down, the yellow leaves were still bright enough to hurt the eye.

Maples leaves turned yellow also, but some turned a vivid red, along with black gums and sourwoods. Hickories were the deepest yellow of all and from the Jim's Knob hillside; I spotted some I hadn't known about. (When squirrels began eating hickory nuts the next August, I tried to remember where they were.)

When holly, ivy, laurel, fir, spruce and pine trees shed last year's, this year's leaves looked greener than at any other time. Some oak leaves didn't at fall at all; they just turned brown and hung on until new buds pushed them off in spring. When an early freeze came, all leaves everywhere went directly to a dull brown and nobody had good color.

With the coming of October, Mother Nature painted every mountain, valley and hillside every color of the rainbow. For a few short days, all trees stood tall in their Sunday best. It was their finest hour, their day in the sun and a grand finale for another season. All too soon, they cried leaves of sadness for a summer gone and all too soon, all stood bare and the Blue Ridge Mountain turned smoky purple in the long sundown shadows. It was a sad time, because another summer had gone south for the winter.

Everybody and everything knew winter was coming and there was a new urgency in the land. Animals ate non-stop: trying to get a head start on the hardest time of the year. With corn to shuck, a hog to kill and tobacco to tie and sell before the market ended, we had our hands full. To add to the aggravation, it took a house full of firewood to keep the house warm all winter and we were already running behind.

As the days grew shorter, the nights grew longer and the stars grew brighter. I counted at least a million, plus or minus a few. The Big Dipper hung high over Sugar Loaf Mountain and shooting stars streaked by. A circle around the moon promised weather, one day in the future for each star inside the circle.

On cooler evenings, we fired up the wood heater and Mama moved her flowerpots into the house: just in case. The late green beans were not quite grown, but with frost in the air one cool evening, we picked them anyway. As Pa said it, "They's stuff to do out yonder ever' which 'a way ya' look and we gotta' gitter' done while we still got time."

Nothing brought home the idea of winter like a heavy frost. They usually began in October and brought a morning coat of white to grass and weeds that had worked overtime-making seeds for next year. Summer's green weeds then dried to brown and rustled in the light breezes. We then dug sweet potatoes and peanuts and picked the last slowpoke tomatoes.

We hauled firewood and pumpkins on the sourwood sled and hunted pine knots in Jim's Knob. We stuffed new straw into the bed ticks, re-stuffed the pillows with "life ever-lasting" and cut broom straw for new brooms. One Indian Summer Day, we gathered black walnuts beside a deep blue Stewart's Creek that mirrored the overhead sky.

With the magic of make-believe, corn shocks became teepees in an Indian village, standing in neat rows across the fields. The Little People of legend rattled dry leaves in moonlit woods and hoot owls called from across the valley. Foxhounds ran in the far Gardner Woods, night birds sang from the river road and the smell of wood smoke and ripe apples came on the night air.

Haystacks stood around stack poles: waiting for young cave makers to tunnel into on cold winter days. I was told, "Don't you go lightin' no matches in there or startin' no fires, or you gonna' see a fire like you ain't never seen before and you won't set down for a week."

With the coming of frost, "simmons" (persimmons) ripened along the rail fence, just waiting for hungry 'possums and me. "Boy, don't you go eatin' none a them 'simmons, a'fore it frosts, or they'll turn your mouth wrong side outards'." They did!

As time dragged on, we hauled unending wagonloads of corn out of Oscar Marshall's creek bottoms and piled it in the middle of the road. On corn-shucking day, we threw a million ears of corn over the pile and threw the shucks behind us. When everything got up to speed, the air was full of flying corn and tall tales, as neighbors swapped the latest gossip and bragged about how good their crops were that year. The best part of the day was the huge corn-shucking dinner Mama cooked; I'd never seen so many pies and cakes.

Blum's Almanac told us how much snow was coming in winter and when to kill the hog. One frosty morning in November, we rolled out of bed at daylight and Pa killed ours with the .22. He cut its throat with a butcher knife so it would "bleed out", while I found other things to do in other places. After rolling the hog into a vat of boiling water, we scraped the hair off with butcher knives and hung it upside down from a tree limb.

After cleaning out the insides, Pa lowered it onto some planks and cut it into pieces with the axe and butcher knife. We "salted-down" the middlins', shoulders and hams, stored them in the granary and made canned sausage.

Mama cooked the fat out of the scrap pieces of meat to make the lard we used for frying all year. Killing hogs was hard, messy work, but it was a necessary part of preparing for winter. With a full meat-box, dried "leather britches" hanging on the back porch, the cellar full of apples and potatoes and the shelves full of canned stuff, no way would we go hungry.

We de-hulled black walnuts and stored them in the granary where the squirrels couldn't get them. De-hulling walnuts brought on a bad case of brown-hand that was hard to wash off. We were told, "Only thing'll take that stuff off is hard work and the way you boys work, it's gonna' take a while."

When one job was finished, two more were waiting to take its place and all had to be done "right now, right this minute." With firewood to cut and tobacco to tie, to say nothing of going to school, we never ran out of jobs.

Every grownup was of the same mind, "We gotta' gitter' done while we still got time, 'cause winter she's a' comin' and she waits for no man." I knew for a fact, we'd never get caught up and never again would we have any time to play.

As the days grew shorter, everybody and everything worked overtime: preparing for a hard winter on Stewart's Creek. Chickens and wild doves scratched in dry grass and leaves, searching for anything that looked like food. Black buzzards floated high overhead as they hunted for something dead. (I never heard of them eating anything alive.) Squirrels built leaf nests in tree forks and hid acorns under fallen leaves. I wondered if they remembered where, when the big snows came.

When we sold tobacco and ivy in the fall, we had more money than at any other time. We "paid-up" Kascos Feed and Seed Store and still had money to buy what we needed, at least what we needed worst. Not owing anybody anything was a great feeling, but we knew it wouldn't last and we'd be broke again.

Warren and I read the Sears Roebuck and Montgomery Ward catalogues from end to end and planned what we'd buy when we got rich. Other than new shoes and school clothes, we got very few new things except at Christmas, but that didn't stop the daydreaming and you could never tell when a miracle might happen.

With some ivy money burning a hole in my pocket, I ordered a brand new mail-order genuine special edition pocket watch, just like the railroad used and tried to meet the mailman every day. When it finally came, the time needed checking every five minutes and it needed winding just as often: two tasks I passed with flying colors. Having money was fun while it lasted, but we knew hard times would come again and when they did, we'd do as we'd always done: we'd do with what we had or we'd do without: which we did.

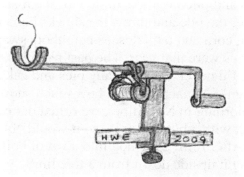

Ivy (mountain laurel)   Ivy stringing machine

With the coming of fall, we headed for the woods with fertilizer sacks to break the ivy we strung at night or on rainy days. One of our favorite places to break it was in the Cleve Thomas Woods. We met a wide-awake copperhead there one cold day that scared me out of my britches. Maybe it lost track of time or found Pa's still place and just didn't care. For whatever reason, it didn't bite anybody and it never made it to hibernation.

With full ivy sacks, we headed for home across the "Low Foot Log" that hung over Stewart's Creek. When out in the middle, it bounced like a rubber ball and the only way to stay on it was to zig when it zagged. Best they could do, some people took an unwanted bath, sometimes a much-needed bath, maybe their only one of the year and sometimes in the coldest weather.

Stringing ivy consisted of placing a small bunch of ivy in the fork at the left end of the ivy machine. (Above right) Turning the crank wrapped wire around bunches of ivy to hold them together and the process continued until the fifty-foot lengths were completed. The T N Woodruff Company at Low Gap then picked them up and sold them to cities all over the United States to decorate the streets for Christmas.

Grandpa's "last"

    After going barefoot all summer, we got new shoes at tobacco selling time. It was our only pair of the year and when holes wore in the soles, Pa "half soled" them on Grandpa's "last" (seen above) with leather and tacks bought at Kasco's. He told us, "You're walking too heavy in them shoes, boys." When Grandpa died, Pa inherited the last and repaired our shoes until there was nothing left to repair. When *Pa* died, I inherited the last and it now sits in my basement, ready to repair shoes, even though shoes are no longer repairable and I don't know how anyway.

    Just north of the Farley Smith and Sid Marshall homes was a huge wooded area called No Man's Land. It was a great place to ramble in the daytime, but unlike the Gardner Woods, it was a little strange. The only signs of people were some old still places and if the place had ever had an owner, nobody knew anything about it. Even it's name made cold chills run all up and down my back.

    When going anywhere alone at night, No Man's Land was the one place I tried not think about and was the one place I thought about most. When anywhere in that area, I kept a sharp lookout behind, just in case something was sneaking up on me.

    I could almost see black-robed witches under the laurel bushes: stirring up a bad brew of bat wings, frogeyes and snake eggs in a big black wash pot under a big yellow moon. I could almost hear their magic words and their crazy cackle. Whatever they were making, it was not for the good of mankind.

    I could also imagine a bootlegger stirring up another type of brew under another laurel thicket. He too wore a black hat and mumbled strange words: his caused by drinking his own moonshine. With Old Betsy handy, he didn't need messing with either.

    A few slugs of moonshine caused some people to see some awesome things that made them run wild through the woods, sometimes in the dark of the moon. That may have been the crashing, thrashing noises people heard at night, including me.

    Running in the dark without a light was not the thing to do, because of all the things you could run into: Demons, trees, briar patches, gullies, barbed wire fences and one another. "Mister, what happened to you? You look like you done tackled a wild cat or run through a bob' wire fence head-foamus."

    I'd heard noises in the dark woods that were heart stopping and I hadn't drunk any moonshine. When it happened, I could easily have put away a gallon all by myself. With no flashlight or lantern, I was too scared to run, so I just stood still, tried to be as small as possible and hoped whatever it was didn't know I was there.

Every stream in No Man's Land drained into Stewart's Creek and eventually into the Atlantic Ocean. Just over the top of Sugar Loaf Mountain, all streams flowed north and west into the New River and eventually into the Mississippi and the Gulf of Mexico.

Since water only ran downhill, I wondered how it got to the top of the mountain in the first place. One theory said water ran uphill at midnight during a Blue Moon, which would explain how it got on top of the mountain, but what happened next? The only place left to go was into the sky, so maybe that was where waterspouts and rain came from. I was a brave soul, but no way would I ever be in such a place at midnight to see if water ran uphill.

One November night, Pa and I went 'possum huntin' in No Man's Land. I was a little leery of being in such a weird place at night, but with him and the lantern along for company, I figured everything would be o k. It would also give me the chance to show him some of my vast scouting know-how: which he'd never seen.

With shotgun, a pocket-full of shells, kerosene lantern and a fertilizer sack to carry the 'possums in, we called the dog and headed for the "Great North Woods" of No Man's Land. Snakes were already gone for the year and with the leaves gone from the trees, it would be easy to see a treed 'possum and shoot it out of the tree.

We headed into the woods beyond Little Sid Marshall's place, as Pa told me about No Man's Land and the "painters" (panthers) that once rode the treetops. The panthers were long-gone, but he said the 'possums in there were just as big and we were about to bring home a "whole sack full." Who'd ever seen a 'possum that big? I could hardly wait!

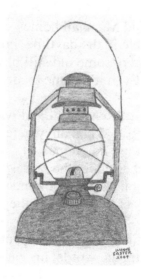

Man's best friend in the woods at night

With the comforting smell of burning kerosene, plenty of light and Pa and his shotgun, there was nothing to fear. We climbed uphill and downhill all over the woods for miles and hours and kept waiting for the dog to strike a 'possum's trail, but that didn't happen. Pa tried to put it on the trail, but "sic em' boy" didn't work anymore. Here was a dog that normally treed everything in sight, but now it didn't like 'possums, or maybe it was just as leery of No Man's Land as me.

At some point, neither of us knew which way to go and cold chills crawled all over me. Here we were lost in No Man's Land: the worst possible place it could happen and chances of anybody finding us were next to none and even less likely at night. The dog was just as lost as us and never got out of our sight. Something had gone badly wrong somewhere and we were in big-time trouble.

Home had never seemed so far away and the woods got bigger and bigger. We rested a while, drank water from a spring branch, tried to decide how many hills we'd climbed, how many branches we'd crossed and how many turns we'd made. Pa thought we needed to go "this-away" and I thought we needed to go "that-away." I couldn't find any moss on the north side of any trees and with clouds hiding the Moon and the North Star; there went any chance of impressing Pa with my deep woods scouting knowledge.

The smell of burning kerosene was comforting, but what if we ran out of oil before we found our way out? No telling what would happen to people in such a place in the middle of the night with no light. Anybody might die before anybody ever found out anybody was missing. I just hoped a hungry panther didn't come along in the treetops.

Pa was my hero, but there were limits to this hero thing and I kept an eye out behind to see if my worst nightmare was sneaking up on us. We heard a foxhunter calling his dogs with a cow horn, "way over yonder somewhere," but we had no idea where that was or in which direction. We wandered around some more, probably in circles and had no idea where we were either. I was tired, hungry, scared and way beyond ready to go home. For certain, 'Possum hunting would never be my thing. Fact of the matter, we'd probably never see daylight again.

We finally heard a big truck climbing Fancy Gap Mountain and knew that was north of No Man's Land. That made home in the opposite direction and I breathed a huge sigh of relief as we headed south. We finally made it back to God's Country and home had never looked so good. We never saw the first 'possum, huge or otherwise, but there was no doubt about them being there because Pa said they were. Never again did we go hunting in No Man's Land.

While walking home one night above the Little Spring, again with no light, I saw something about as big as me lying on the road bank, glowing with a cold blue fire. My hair headed for the sky and my chill bumps took off through the woods.

I'd seen stuff shining in the dark before: wildfire in the mountain, heat lightning, the Northern Lights, lightning bugs, glow worms and an orange sky when the old Beulah School burned. None of those compared with whatever it was shining beside the road.

I stood very still and hoped it wasn't as bad as it looked and after another silent conversation with the Lord, a tiny bit of courage came back. A lit match in shaking hands showed me an old rotten log lying beside the road, glowing cold blue. I took a piece of it home and it still glowed. (I later learned it was foxfire: something I'd never heard about.)

Someone told about a man going home in the dark with no lantern: the usual situation for scary tales. A "painter" (panther) had been seen in the area and in the man's mind, there was behind every bush, just waiting to pounce.

Somehow a ball of twine in his coat pocket began unrolling and catching in the dry leaves behind him. When he heard the noise, he knew for sure: a panther was creeping up on him. He ran a short distance with the noise following behind and when he stopped to listen, the noise stopped. When he ran again, the noise ran too and the faster he ran, the faster the noise ran. He ran all the way home, fell in the door and said, "They's a painter after me."

Such were the things I thought of when going anywhere alone in the dark with no light. No matter how positive I was that nothing was out there, the more positive I was that something was.

October was long gone from our Blue Ridge Mountains, as another season came to an end. The tired fields of summer were finally at rest and we were rolling downhill on a long journey into winter. Night came early and we could never get all the chores done before dark.

One late fall day, we sawed firewood in the South Forty Woods, as high thin clouds came up in the western sky: foretelling coming weather, "tomorrow for sure," according to Pa. As the sun went behind Fisher's Peak, we called it a day and headed home as a big Hunter's Moon came up over the trees. When we came around the last curve, the smell of wood smoke came on the night air and yellow lamplight in the window promised safety and warmth in the long winter nights that would soon be coming over that mountain back yonder.

Home

Winter on the Blue Ridge Parkway 1971

Chapter 17

Late fall

November (1970s)

Summer had already gone south, so fast it didn't seem possible. The old folks told me again, "You think time's a' flyin' now, boy, you ain't seen nothin' yet." The leaves were gone from the trees and we could once again see Sugar Loaf Mountain from the front porch: now a deep blue instead of green, as it had been all summer. We could again see Little Sid Marshall's house across the valley and see smoke climb into the sky from Grandpa's chimney, unless weather was coming, then it stayed low in the valley.

That salet patch was the only thing still growing and we sent the little green worms that ate on it to "you know where" with the bean duster. (Nothing, but nothing messed with our curly-leaf mustard and turnip greens.) The turnips were good too, but when I fed one to the horse, its mouth got into an impossible shape, the same shape it got into when I fed it a crayon: "wrong-side-outards."

Pa fall-plowed the garden and potato patches to "lay over the winter." which improved the land and "froze out all them cussed varmints." It didn't work very well, because we still had an army of bean beetles, cucumber beetles, cut worms, tobacco worms, moles, squash bugs and flea-bugs every summer. All those ate on the crops and everything else ate on me.

In spite of stray animals, frost, drought, hail, wind and a sneaky neighbor, we had no crop failures and thanks to the food Mama canned, stored and dried in summer, we we never went hungry. It was sad when the garden died back in fall, but at least the varmints quit eating me alive.

The first morning frost brought the first fire in the heater and turned the yard grass bright white. "Got a young snow out there this mornin', boys; I tracked myself all the way to the barn." As the days grew shorter, the nights grew longer and dark came earlier: long before we got the chores done. We now knew for sure, winter was coming and we headed for the South Forty woods to cut a house full of firewood.

We cut green firewood on our own land but dry dead wood came from anywhere we found it. No matter where it came from, the heater and cook stove burned wood like it was free and regardless of how much we cut ahead of time, it was never enough. It was said a house-full of wood just might keep a house warm all winter and I was a believer.

When not sawing firewood, we almost lived in Grandpa's pack house basement, trying to get all the tobacco tied and sold before the buying season ended. No way could we afford to carry any tobacco over 'til next year. It was the one time of year when we had more to do than an army could do, to say nothing of summer and spring and any other time, for that matter.

Rabbit gum

Beginning in October, we set rabbit gums, a practice almost as important as squirrel hunting. People with access to sawmills made gums from planks, which looked more "store-boughten," but ours were made from three-foot sections of a hollow log, just like Grandpa's. They blended into the landscape better and worked just like the plank gums. I don't think rabbits cared either way, as long as they found an apple inside.

We baited the gums, set them along pathways and checked each day to see if we'd caught anything. When the trap door was down, there was almost always a rabbit, 'possum or something inside. Some people caught polecats and when they did, you knew it long before they got close and they had no close friends until the smell went away.

By the end of November, we'd shucked the corn, killed the hog and had enough food in the basement to feed everybody on Earth for a year. We were far from being caught up, but the longer nights gave me more time to read unless we ran out of kerosene oil; then we went to bed with the chickens.

A fur company ad promised big money for animal hides and with eyes as big as saucers, my fortune was assured. All I had to do was run a trap line all winter, catch some minks, foxes and raccoons and the big money would come rolling in. Never again would I have to hoe corn and tobacco in hot summer fields and sweat my life away.

I was already a great hunter, so why not get rich at the same time? I'd probably catch so many animals they'd have to be hauled home on the sled and I'd be up all night skinning minks (which brought the most money) and mounting their hides on boards to dry. I might even have to whittle out more boards. With all that money, I could buy everything in the Sears Roebuck and Montgomery Ward catalogues.

Grandpa helped me set some old steel traps along the creek banks and told me about the animals and birds, what they ate and where they lived. He told about the good old days and all the years he'd farmed, what kind of tree that was and when it was going to snow. He knew all the important things and tried to answer all of my questions.

He told about wild turkey hunts in the Tom Hawks Woods and driving his wagon on Stewart's Creek when it froze over. "Sometimes we got snowed in for weeks, because winters was rougher back then and it was so cold we never got away from the fire." (Why couldn't I have lived back in the good old days?)

I walked for miles in the Great North Woods that winter and could see dollar signs around every creek bend. Even in the blinding wind snow, I could hardly wait to get to the next trap, hoping I'd caught something.

Running a successful trap line required some wading with Pa's knee-length rubber boots and a a slippery underwater rock near Grandpa's bottom caused a boot full of "Far North" icy creek-water. I'd already been told, "If you don't drown down yonder in that creek, son, you gonna' freeze to death." When the boot filled up with ice water, I thought I was about to do both and instantly came face to face with Grandpa's good old days. Nobody had told me they'd ever made anything that cold.

Pa had said, "You boys ain't got sense enough to pour pee out of a boot with the directions on the heel." I proved him wrong and broke all records getting out of the creek and emptying the boot. Compared to the icy water, the cold air was so warm I almost cried.

As with most of my earth-shaking projects, imagination exceeded reality, but I finally caught two muskrats along the creek banks. The first one had drowned, but the next one was still alive in shallow water and after dreading it for a while, I finally drowned it with a stick.

I skinned those two: along with a few rabbits and possums and dried all the hides on wooden boards. I mailed everything away and the $12.00 check that came back was the most money I'd ever had. Even so, I decided there were easier ways to make money: like grubbing stumps, sawing wood with a crosscut saw and hoeing corn and tobacco in hot summer fields.

Thanksgiving Day came with carloads of kinfolks and Mama cooked another corn-shucking dinner. With so many people talking at the same time, nobody could hear what anybody said. Everybody bragged about their great kids and the great crop year: how many hound dogs they had, how good they were and how much canned stuff they'd put up. Who cared about all that stuff? I hadn't had anything to eat for at least a week and thought dinnertime would never come.

Just at the point of total starvation, the grown-ups gathered around the table and the kids gathered everywhere else. The table was loaded and we ate chicken and dumplings, deviled eggs, cakes, apple and pumpkin pies and all kinds of good stuff. It was every man for him-self and every man dived in, along with every woman and everybody else. If anybody left the table hungry, no way was it about to be me. Mama had done herself proud.

The women cleaned up the table, washed dishes, dipped snuff and gossiped about the women not there. The younger kids played hide and seek, the older girls talked about boys, while the older boys hid behind the barn, smoked rabbit tobacco and talked about girls.

The grown-up men gathered shotguns, rifles, dogs, a fruit jar of moonshine and headed out for the traditional Thanksgiving Day rabbit hunt. It was a rite of passage for older young men and "Nobody what don't like huntin' ain't right in the head"

Shotguns soon boomed all over the country: sounding like squirrel hunting time in late summer. Anybody running a still within five miles was soon running for his life, somewhere in the next county: figuring the law was headed straight for his still.

Every hunter had the "best durn huntin' dog God ever made." "Ol' Blue's the best fox-hound anybody ever knowed tell of. I'll put 'im up against any dog what's ever been. One time, he run a fox for two days and nights and never got tired. They run plumb into Round Peak, Skull Camp and back around Flower Gap and I nearly had to shoot 'im to git 'im stopped."

No animal or bird was safe on Thanksgiving Day and most of the hunters came home with something: bobwhites, squirrels or rabbits. Some sampled the moonshine and forgot all about hunting. They had the best time of all and came home with red faces. "That there's snake-bite medicine, son. Even right here in the middle of winter, you can't never tell when one of them hibernatin' copperheads'll come crawlin' back outta' the ground and you gotta' be ready."

By mid-December, the pace had slowed down considerably. We were no longer dying in the hot summer fields, the tobacco was sold, the bills were paid and we had money again. After going barefoot all summer, we had new shoes and one tobacco-selling day around 1940; I ate my first hamburger on Market Street in Mt Airy. It was right up there with fried chicken.

With the big rush finally over, we had time to think again and there was great satisfaction in knowing we'd done our best. We'd followed the moon signs like God intended and we'd had a good year. With the basement full of can-stuff, the granary full of corn, fatback and walnuts and a barn full of animal food, nobody or nothing would go hungry on our hill. The wolf would have to find himself another door to scratch at.

As the year deepened into winter, young people's minds turned to Christmas, Santa Clause and trying to be good. We searched far woods, found a small cedar tree, nailed a plank on the bottom and placed it in front of the window for a Christmas tree. We decorated it with paper chains, popcorn on a string and made wreaths of running cedar and holly and hung them where Santa would be sure to see them. With craft paper from school, flour paste glue and scissors, we made Christmas cards for Santa and everybody in the family.

We wore the Sears Roebuck and Montgomery Ward catalogues dog-eared and bent certain people's ears, telling them about all the great things Santa would bring. It was great to daydream and you could never tell when a miracle might happen.

Just like every year, we were told, "Things ain't lookin' good this year boys and Santa may not come at all, so don't expect much." Our thinking, "But we've been good this whole year and he's gottta' come." Surely Santa would remember all that water we toted from the spring, all that stove wood we toted in, all them chickens we fed, all them times we slopped the hog and all them miles of corn rows we hoed.

We didn't have much worth stealing on our hill and never locked the doors. All of a sudden, we began doing so: especially at night. Maybe we had valuables I didn't know about, because Pa began locking the granary door about the same time. (Actually, he'd found a new place to stash his jug.)

Everybody knew how Santa worked, he came streaking across the sky from the North Pole, landed on the roof, came down the chimney and in through the fireplace. We had a small chimney for the heater and a stovepipe for the cook stove but no fireplace.

On top of that, the chimney was too small for even an ordinary person, let alone somebody as big as Santa. With a too-little chimney, no fireplace and all the doors locked, we had a big problem. If I ever had a house, I'd have a big chimney, a huge fireplace, no door locks and maybe no doors.

Pa didn't help matters any, "If Santa comes down my chimney, I'm gonna' shoot 'im with my shotgun." I almost believed him because the shotgun was very much a part of our lives. When neighbors shot firecrackers at Christmas, (which we couldn't afford) Pa answered with the shotgun and yelled, "Hurrah for Doc Hatfield, by dotey. Whoopee." (I never knew what he might say or do next.) One thing for sure, if I ever had a house, I'd have no shotgun and Santa would be always be welcome

Hellfire and Damnation

As the days dragged on, I tried to forget about Christmas, because with the chimney too small and all the other problems, it didn't matter much anyway. Then, to top it all, along came something even worse.

One dark dreary day, what little peace and quiet we had jumped out the window and headed for the hills. Wearing black hats, black beards and red faces, Hellfire and Damnation came roaring down the hill in a muddy open top black "skeeter": looking something like the above. It spewed a white cloud of radiator steam into the air, backfired all the way and sounded like a war had begun. It was the most terrifying sight I'd ever seen.

(A preacher had told us he was making a Christian Endeavor to get people to go to his new church and us being experts on big words; we figured he meant "Christian Devil." We decided right away, "We ain't goin' to no church with none of them Christian Devils.") When the calamity came roaring down the hill, two of them appeared right before my very eyes.

I knew right away we'd made the wrong decision about church and there'd be "you-know-what" to pay. I was already being good for Christmas and bad things were not supposed to happen to good guys like me. It was easy to see that something had gone badly wrong somewhere and right at Christmas time. Going to church next Sunday now seemed like a great idea, but Sunday was days away and this was now and it was way too late to run.

I watched from behind the house as the skeeter clattered to a stop, made one last loud bang and sat there spewing steam. Instead of Christian Devils, they were two of the meanest looking people I'd ever seen. Real devils with pitchforks wouldn't have scared me any worse.

They had a shotgun, a big pistol and a jug of moonshine for snakebites and were ready for Freddy and everybody else. It was said moonshine would cure any ailment known to mankind, including cold weather, snakebites, bad luck and bad news. Whatever the case, those two were loaded for bear and feared no man.

I couldn't see any pitchforks or red tails, so maybe they were not quite as bad as they looked. As it came to be, they were two of Pa's drinking buddies from "over yonder in Gyarbrawley," as he called it. When they offered Pa a sample from the fruit jar, he took no chances on snakes and told them, "You all light and come in."

I never knew if their red faces were caused by the cold or the moonshine, but they were getting a head start on Christmas and feeling no pains. After passing the fruit jar around a few times, Pa was feeling no pains either. They all had a great time telling tall tales and trying to shoot the top out of a white pine tree with the pistol.

With all the smoke, noise, and commotion, I knew Santa would never come to our house again. They drank a while, laughed a while, sang a while and shot the pistol. The tree was never in much danger, but Little Sid Marshall was in the line of fire and they were shooting straight toward his house across the valley.

After what seemed like forever, the moonshine ran out and they went chic-a-lacking back up the hill to wherever they came from. The next time I heard a car coming, I hid behind the house again and peeped around the corner again.

After half a lifetime of waiting, Christmas Eve finally came and I watched the sky toward the North Star, because that was where Santa came from. I could almost see him up there among the stars and knew he had to be a fast mover to visit every house in the world in one night.

Just thinking about all those toys put magic in the air and Warren and I tried to stay up all night to see what happened. "You'd better git to sleep, boys, 'cause Santa ain't comin' 'til you do." It was very hard to go to bed, but somehow, someway, far in the night, we slept.

Christmas was the only day of the year when nobody had to chase us out of bed and we came out at daylight. It was a rat race to the tree to see if Santa had made it down our chimney. Just like we'd known he'd do all along, he'd made it and we had apples, oranges, candy and new toys.

We didn't exactly get everything in the Sears Roebuck catalogue, but what we got was worth the waiting and anticipation. Since we'd been little angels for weeks, we'd known all along he wouldn't forget good kids like us. "See? I told you he'd come."

With new toys on hand, there was almost no time for breakfast and chores, but after being threatened with a good dose of hickory tea, we worked everything into our busy schedule.

One special Christmas, Santa brought a pair of six shooters on a gun belt and Wild Bill Easter headed west. While practicing fast-draw, one of the guns broke and being made of sawdust and glue, I taped and glued it back together and it wiped out the outlaws just like before.

Kinfolks came for Christmas dinner and we ate chicken and dumplings, homemade pies and a fruitcake and everybody ate like it was their last meal. When everybody was stuffed, the women washed dishes, swapped the latest gossip and recipes and bragged about their smart kids. The younger kids played with new toys, played house, fought corncob wars and played cowboys and Indians. Just like always, the older boys hid behind the barn, smoked rabbit tobacco and talked about girls.

The men headed for the granary to do some long-range weather forecasting. With a full jug of moonshine hidden inside, the process took a while. They did most of the heavy work inside, but came outside often to check the sky and wind direction. As the day wore on, they became happier and happier and the weather reports got better and better. Long before the day ended, they had decided next year would be an outstanding year.

Just like Foot-washing Day at Crooked Oak Church, time raced by on Christmas Day and all too soon, the sun went down behind Fisher's Peak and everybody went home. It was such a sad time, because we'd had such a great time on a day that should never have ended. Why couldn't everyday be Christmas?

The coldest part of the year was now at hand, bringing snow; sleet, freezing rain and wind that blew for weeks on end. Nothing to eat grew outside, but thanks to the hard work we'd done all summer, we would not go hungry. A whole new year was coming and I for one, was ready for one of Grandpa's "ole timey" January Winters: when "you know what froze over."

As the year came to an end, winter began playing for keeps in the high hills and deep valleys. The tin roof rattled all night long, as the wind moaned around the house eaves. With anticipation and dread, I watched Sugar Loaf Mountain turn dark blue in the bitter cold, as the whole world took a deep breath and dived into the coldest part of the year.

The fields of winter (1970s)

The green fields of summer were now the brown fields of winter and bare tree limbs searched for the sun in a cold sky. Unlike before Christmas, the pine and cedar trees were dull and lifeless and the whole world had gone to sleep: just waiting for what would soon be coming "over that mountain back yonder."

On the last day of the year, the old hunter was home from the far hills: warm and sleepy in his place by the fire. He had done his best all year and was content. No more fields would be ploughed this year and the harvest was complete for man and beast. For better or worse, another year had come and gone like so many others: never to come again.

Now was a time to rest and be thankful for all the many blessings: a time to doze, a time to dream and remember yesterday, when he was younger and had the world by the tail with a downhill drag. There was a time when he could plough the fields from sunup to sundown, square dance all night, and run the creek banks in all kinds of weather.

He knew those days would not come again, but with a stack of firewood, shelter and a full meat box, he was at peace and knew if the sun came up tomorrow, it would be another good day and a brand new year.

The mists of time

Epilogue

Grow old along with me: the best is yet to be.

Somewhere there is a river of time and memory, where the morning sun still comes up over Dave Carson's bottoms, warming newly ploughed land, as ploughmen of old follow mules and horses forever across endless fields. All who ever lived on Stewart's Creek are still there: working the cornfields of their ancestors, raising families and helping their neighbors in times of need.

From sunup to sundown, they follow the unending rows, planting, chopping, plowing and gathering: just as their parents and grandparents did before them. Their sweat, blood and tears have drowned the land for generations and they are the stronger for it. All are living each day as best they know how: digging a living from the Earth and planning for a hard winter. Unending faith promises them another day tomorrow and it will be a good one.

Far in the backwoods, barefoot children and their dogs run wild along the ridgelines, searching for high adventure. The whole world is as new as this morning: a huge, exciting place with unending wonders. There will never be enough time to see it all, but they will give it a good try. No matter how far they ramble or how long they're gone, they know a warm home and supper will be waiting at the end of the day.

On a far hillside, a squirrel hunter dozes under a hickory tree, as the world goes by down below. With muzzleloader by his side, he is primed and ready, just in case a squirrel comes by. After a long hot summer in the cornfields, it's great to relax and daydream about all the good things in life: like supper, squirrel dumplings, buckwheat pancakes and white sop gravy.

Far down in the valley, his wife hangs freshly washed clothes on the garden fence clothesline, as the fire dies down under the black wash pot they were boiled in. With so many jobs to be done, her life is hard and her days are long. Like every other woman on Stewart's Creek, she'll do what has to be done and when the sun finally goes down behind the mountain, supper will be waiting for her family.

Pa sits on the front porch of his log cabin home in the springtime woods: watching the trees turn green, "The fastest I ever seen." He sings his favorite song, "Oh, they tell me of a home where no storm clouds rise. Oh, they tell me of an un-cloudy day." He pats his foot and plays his French harp just like DeFord Baily did on Jim Smith's battery-powered radio in 1938.

Thanks to his sons, he no longer cuts his own firewood and thanks to Mama, supper will be waiting at the end of the day. With a pack of "seegars," a jug of moonshine in the granary and a Social Security check coming in the mail, he is a rich man.

On snowy winter mornings, he keeps the home-fires burning, as Mama cooks breakfast. He tunes the radio loudly to WJJD Chicago for another weather forecast. His weather report tells one and all in no uncertain terms, "It's cold as Hell out there in Chicago." As he has done many times before, he passes on a bit of wisdom to his sons, "It takes money to drink liquor and ride the train, boys."

Mama sits contentedly by the warm wood heater and dips her Square brand snuff. She hums a tune, sews quilt pieces and thinks about the good old days. When the kids were young, her days were filled with things that absolutely had to be done and done right now. Her work was never done except late at night when all the boys were fed and put to bed. Only then was there time to hope and pray that nobody got hurt or sick. Come tomorrow, she would start all over again and cook breakfast for a starving family. With all the food she had canned and stored in the basement, nobody would go hungry at her house.

With the kids now gone from home, she no longer stays up half the night replacing lost shirt buttons and patching worn out overalls. Finally, at long last, she has time to relax, think about the past and the good old days and wonder what would be good for supper.

Grandpa sits in his tack room repairing broken leather harness that has been repaired many times before. His worn-out saddle, horse-collar, plow lines and singletree have also seen better days, but they still do the job.

From lifelong habit, he scans the sky for a weather forecast, peels an apple, hums a folk song and tries to answer my all of my many questions. He sorts through a never-ending list of things to do: today, tomorrow and next week, but as for right now, all the crops are in, the tobacco is sold, the hog is killed, he has winter firewood and all is well with the world.

It has been a long hard summer, but with never-ending faith in the future, he knows the rains will come at the right time and next year will be another good crop year. Whatever happens tomorrow, he will be ready and waiting when the sun comes up over Gardner's Ridge.

A cowbell clangs in the hillside pasture, reminding him that milking time is coming and Stewart's Creek sings a fishing song as it runs the rapids a half a mile down the valley.

Grandma sits in her cane bottom chair: churning butter in a wooden churn, as corn bread bakes in a Dutch Oven in the fire place ashes. She will pack the butter into a wooden mold that makes a pretty leaf-print on it and come Saturday, Grandpa will fire up his one-horse wagon and sell it at Kasco's on Market Street in Mt Airy.

A glass cake dish on the kitchen table contains half a homemade cake I can smell a mile away. Come tomorrow, she will make homemade soap from meat scraps, Red Devil Lye and fireplace ashes. "That stuff'll eat your hands up, boy."

As another summer day comes to an end, a full moon comes up over the Cleve Thomas Road, as a whippoorwill calls from the Little Bottom and another answers from the pasture hill. Foxhounds run in the far Gardner Woods, a mocking bird sings from atop the Big John Apple tree and tree frogs call for rain. The last light of day brings peace; the cow is milked, the animals are fed and a night of rest will bring rest and strength, so the old folks can face another brand new day tomorrow.

From the front porch of a log cabin home, an old couple watches the trees change color in October hillsides. They no longer get around too well, but thanks to caring neighbors, they have firewood for the coming winter and food in the basement. They know when the big snows come in January, they'll be warm and fed and content.

Jim Smith's log wine barn on Pine Ridge Road

   An old man with a long white beard sits by his roaring fireplace in a hundred-year-old cabin: watching the world go by in the flames. With cane and dog by his side, a sack of pinto beans, corn meal, a middling of meat and a stack of winter firewood, he is content. The dog is his best friend and second best is his memory: bringing back the good old days when he owned the world.
   He has seen the wild geese fly north in February for more years than he can remember. He has chopped the wood, plowed the land, sowed the seeds, fished every river and climbed every mountain, but those days, like so many seasons and so many friends, have come and gone, never to return. Spring, summer and fall are gone again and the popping sounds in the fire tell of coming winter storms, when the whole country will be covered with snow. Whatever comes tomorrow, he will be ready and waiting when the sun comes up.
   On the same river of time, memory takes me back to the Nineteen Forties when the world was big, wide and wonderful and all mine. I can again burn the midnight oil, while learning to read by the light of a kerosene lamp. There was adventure around every bend in the road, a whole lifetime ahead and everybody I knew would be there forever. Tomorrow was coming in the morning and like Grandpa, I knew it would be another great day.

Made in the USA
Monee, IL
15 November 2023

46601812R00096